Free
Yourself
of
Everything

Free Yourself
of
Everything

Radical Guidance in the
Spirit of Zen and
Christian Mysticism

Wolfgang Kopp

translated from the German by
Barbara Wittenberg-Hasenauer

CHARLES E. TUTTLE CO., INC
BOSTON • RUTLAND, VERMONT • TOKYO

First English language edition published 1994 by
Charles E. Tuttle Company, Inc.
of Rutland, Vermont & Tokyo, Japan, with editorial offices at
153 Milk Street, Boston, Massachusetts 02109

German language edition published in 1991 by
Ansata-Verlag, Interlaken,© 1991 Wolfgang Kopp

Library of Congress Cataloging-in-Publication Data

Kopp, Wolfgang, 1938-
    [Befreit euch von allem. English]
    Free yourself of everything : radical guidance in the spirit
of Zen and Christian mysticism / by Wolfgang Kopp ;
translated from the German by Barbara Wittenberg-
Hasenauer.
             p. cm.
    1. Spiritual life—Zen Buddhism. 2. Mysticism—
Comparative studies. 3. Zen Buddism—Relations—
Christianity. 4. Christianity and other religions—Zen
Buddhism. I. Title.
BQ9268.6.K6614 1994
294.3'444—dc20   94-7393
                                          CIP

ISBN 0-8048-1989-0
Text design by Jill Winitzer

First Edition
3 5 7 9 10 8 6 4 2
(TP)

Printed in the United States of America

Contents

In Reverence to Soji Enku Roshi

Translator's Note

Wolfgang Kopp was born in Wiesbaden, Germany in
1938. In his early years he tread many different paths in
search of the truth, such as philosophy, Hinduism, and
Tibetan Buddhism. The first time he visited the dojo (meditation
hall) of his Zen master, Soji Enku Roshi, he knew instantly that
his search was over.

As Soji Enku Roshi's dharma successor, Wolfgang Kopp directs
the Tao Ch'an Center in Wiesbaden. He is one of the few genuine
Western spiritual masters of our times. His teaching embraces the
true mysticism of all ages and cultures, but is especially grounded
in the Zen of the ancient Chinese masters of the Tang dynasty,
such as Ma-tsu, Pai-chang, Huang-po, and Lin-chi, and in the
Christian mysticism of his landsman, Meister Eckhart.

While reading this book you may be struck by the authoritative
tone of the author's writing. It is helpful to keep in mind that this
authority is bred of the experience of the highest truth and has no
other purpose than to direct readers to the ultimate realization of
their true self.

As Master Kopp's translator and Zen student, I am grateful for
his guidance in assisting me with this work and for the opportunity it has given me to deepen my understanding of Zen. I have done
my best to preserve the colorful expressions, sense of humor, and
intensity of his writing; and hope that the directness, compassion,
and wisdom of his teaching will be felt by all who turn to his
words.

Foreword

There are no living beings
that cannot be freed.
                    —Lin-chi

Interest in Western and Eastern mysticism has grown remarkably in recent years. In these times of spiritual reflection, it is of utmost importance that the way that leads humanity to the direct experience of its true self is clearly conveyed.

This book was written in consideration of the needs of serious spiritual seekers, to disclose to them a safe, albeit radical way to self-knowledge and thus to freedom. Whoever takes this book in hand should understand that it is not meant to be merely read, but instead to be thoroughly contemplated and lived. Only to this end were its contents written, and only in this sense can it be absorbed. This work is not pleasure reading, but a guide to within.

The title of the book, Free Yourself of Everything, originates from a saying of the Chinese Zen master, Huang-po (9th century). The expression, "free yourselves of everything," like Christian mysticism's "die and come into being," constitutes the central thought of this book. The subtitle, Radical Guidance in the Spirit of Zen and Christian Mysticism, refers to the consistent application of this central thought.

It is clear to me that this book is an enormous challenge for the reader's ego-this was intended. The intention was to shake the ego to its very foundation and rouse the reader, so that by becoming completely engaged in the book, the reader may find himself or herself a different person at the end of the reading.

From my own experience, as well as from many years of guiding students, I know that without consistency, progress on the spiritual way is impossible. With this in mind, the present book is addressed to all earnest spiritual seekers who have a sincere longing for consistent, yet safe spiritual guidance.

This book seeks to help find the inner source; its aim is to lead truth-seekers to that extraordinary experience of realization, where book-learning is replaced by experience, knowledge is replaced by the wisdom of the heart, and the belief in a merely conceptual God is replaced by the enlightenment of your own mind.

—Wolfgang Kopp
Wiesbaden, October 1990

Mind is filled with radiant clarity,
so cast away the darkness of your old concepts.
Free yourselves of everything.
— Huang-po

CHAPTER ONE

The Universality of the Mind

THE WORLD IS AN ILLUSION

In the darkness of the heart, in our innermost self, shines a radiant light, the very same as the eternal flame that illuminates the entire universe. This, our true being, is the absolute reality underlying all we experience. As the pure original source of all being, it is unborn and indestructible. It neither comes nor goes; it is ever-present, still and pure, and outside of space and time.

Our original divine nature is, however, covered up at all times by a multitude of passions and imaginings. The uninterrrupted flow of concepts continuously fabricated by our intellects and deep-rooted habits of thinking casts a dark shadow over our true self. Fascinated by this spectacle taking place on the surface of our consciousness, we are incapable of freeing ourselves from it and thus find ourselves in a state of confusion and clouding of the mind. We are held captive by our own projections and believe them to be a reality that exists separately from us.

Blinded by this misperception, we are no longer able to perceive the spiritual magnificence of our divine being and thus wander lost in samsara, the cycle of life and death. Trapped in the dream of an imaginary, multitudinous world, we have lost ourselves and no longer know who we are. Since our dream-wandering is only a

1

vision, we are unable to confirm the actuality of any occurrence. We indeed believe that we live in a three-dimensional, multitudinous world of space and time; yet in reality only the mind moves. Mind is the foundation of everything; samsara takes place in the mind only. The entire universe in its endless diversity and all forms of life are none other than mind.

In Ashvaghosha's *Shraddhotpada-shastra* (Awakening of Faith), a Buddhist work of the 2nd century, it says:

> All things in the world are unreal and illusory; they are only projections of the mind. Apart from the mind there are no objects (of sensory perception). What does this mean? This means that—since all phenomena are projected by the mind and its deluded thoughts—all distinctions are in fact acts of distinguishing one's own mind. But the (ordinary, individual intellect) mind cannot see the (universal, cosmic) mind. Therefore, one should know that all objects and experiences of this world are sustained only by men's ignorant and deluded minds. Just like the images reflected from a mirror, all things are devoid of a true entity; they are false, illusory, and of "mind-only," because only when mind arises do all things arise; when the mind stops its functioning, all things also cease to exist.[1]

Everything that we perceive in the world, including the apparent solidity of matter, is subsequently no more than the illusory imagining of the mind. The mind is the creator of all things. And since our body is also a part of this world, we must consequently conclude that it, as well, is no more than an idea. Our body is simply the visible manifestation of a prior consciousness, formed by the particular inclinations of a former life. Its apparent materiality and solidity is an illusion based on the incredibly quick movement of its atomic components, which should naturally be viewed as purely mental as well. The illusion of the stability of material is similar to the illusion of an impenetrable disc created by the movement of a rapidly turning propeller.

The dynamic nature of the universe extends itself from the atom to the vast dimensions of the galaxies. Everything is in continuous motion, which ultimately takes place in the mind only. Its nature is to manifest itself in myriad arising and subsiding forms. These are in a constant state of fluctuation, endlessly taking on different forms. The objects of our perception may appear passive and lifeless to the naked eye; yet if I were, for example, to examine under a microscope the pencil that I hold in my hand, its dynamic nature would be revealed. In truth, I cannot even say that it is a solid object; it is much more a series of fluctuating occurrences—occurrences that take place in the mind. Mind is the foundation of everything; all things exist in it, and nothing at all exists outside of mind.

In the *Lankavatara Sutra*, one of the most important texts of Mahayana Buddhism, it is thus stated:

> What appears to be external does not exist in reality; it is indeed mind that is seen in in multiplicity; the body, property and the world—all these, I say, are nothing but mind.
> That which can take something and that which is taken—all these, I say, are nothing but mind. . . .
> Apart from mind, nothing whatsoever exists![2]

What we generally define as the reality of our external world actually has no more substance than an image in a dream.

Asanga's compendium of Mahayana doctrine (*Mahayana-sam-parigraha-shastra*) explains:

> With what metaphors can we illustrate the principle of the teaching of mind-only? With the dream and the dreamer. This is to say that all dream-visions do not truly exist; they are but manifestations of the mind. Although various forms, sounds, smells, touches, houses, woods, mountains . . . are projected therein, they are not truly existent. With this metaphor one can understand that in all times and places, all things are but the mind. . . .
> When one reaches enlightenment, or when true wisdom is awakened, he will then come to this realization. This is just the same as when one does not realize the nature of a dream while he is dreaming. By the same token, when one has not yet awakened from the dream of samsara, a full realization of the truth of mind-only will not come to him.[3]

The only world we can speak of at all is the world of our experience. And if we think we can establish the actual existence of the external world through sensual perception, we are mistaken. The only thing we can actually prove is the functional ability of our senses. Everything we label as matter is simply a dimension of the mind we define by resistance, form, visibility, and the like. In reality it is impossible for us to come in contact with the objects of our perception. We can only describe touch sensations, feel resistance, see forms, etc., all of which have nothing at all to do with matter itself, but result rather from a number of sense perceptions we have identified with the concept of matter.

What this ultimately means is that since we perceive the world only by means of our senses and consciousness, we are forced to acknowledge that we can only speak of our subjectively experienced world as a concept. In other words: "The world is no more than our own conception."

THE ILLUSION OF MULTIPLICITY

Everything we perceive in the manifold world is an idea, a conception of our mind, which yet is not created by our individual mind. The individual mind is better understood as a participant, that is, the ideas of material objects are given to it. Since there are really no different kinds of minds, we must concede that the many individual minds are a fictitious and therefore illusory part of an indivisible mind. For if the mind present in each individual were a unique mind, it would be impossible for two people to perceive the same world in the same way. Each individual mind would have its own different perception of the world, distinct from that of all other individual minds. But since all multitudinous perceptions are illusions caused by our spiritual blindness, we must conclude that there can only be a sole being, a single self that is the sole reality of the one mind, instead of unique, separate, independent, individual selves. Let us illustrate this point.

Imagine that we are iridescent soap bubbles floating in infinite space. The inner and outer domain of each soap bubble is the boundless, endless expanse of space. Even if a hundred, thousand, or a hundred thousand soap bubbles were to occupy this endless expanse, we would still be unable to confirm the existence of a multitude of individual spaces. Each differentiation of space

4

would only be an apparent one. In reality there is only the one endless expanse of the universe. Yet each soap bubble within this expanse, out of ignorance resulting from the clouding of the mind, believes itself to possess its own unique inner space and sees itself as one of many separate, individual soap bubbles. But if suddenly all the bubbles were to burst, nothing would remain but the one boundless reality of the universe.

This metaphor illustrates that the perception arising from our senses and intellect of a multitudinous world is an illusion and therefore a misperception. The world as seen by the average person is thus a perception of the indivisible being limited by ego-consciousness and misinterpreted as multiplicity. Ego-consciousness acts like a magician, permitting us to experience a world that actually does not exist. Blinded by the illusion of a supposed multitudinous world, we are unable to recognize our true self as the divine reality underlying all we experience.

As we detach ourselves from all external phenomena and turn increasingly toward the inner light of the mind, we will come to know our true self as the self that is common to all beings. In the words of the wise seer Vamadeva in the *Brihadaranyaka Upanishad*, one of India's holy scriptures, we will then be able to declare:

> I am the self of all of mankind, as well as of the sun. Therefore, now also, whoever realizes Brahman knows that he himself is the self in all creatures. Even the gods cannot harm such a man, since he becomes their innermost self. Now if a man worship Brahman, thinking Brahman is one and he another, he has not the true knowledge.[4]

The omnipresence of divine being pervades the entire universe.

All fluctuation and change is God's progressive self-unfolding and self-transformation; it is realization of the inexpressible divine ground. The entire endless diversity of the external phenomenal world is ultimately the manifestation of this one all-embracing mind and thus the universe is its revelation. As Indian philosophy puts it, the universe is "exhaled" from mind over the unimaginably long time span of a *mahamanvantara*, only to be inhaled again over an equally long period of rest. The Hindu tradition refers to this as Brahman's resting and dreaming.

If Brahman rests in a dreamless sleep, there is no universe. There are no manifold phenomena; there is no thought, and no individual consciousness. Only the single pure consciousness of the one mind remains. If Brahman begins to dream, the whole universe with its phenomena arises in the dream. In the *Bhagavad-Gita*, considered the gospel of Hinduism, Lord Krishna describes the rhythmic cycle of creation with the following words:

> At the end of the night of time all things return to my nature, and when the new day of time begins, I bring them again to the light. Thus through my nature I bring forth all creation, and this rolls about in the circles of time. But I am not bound by my act of creation. I am, and I watch the drama of the works.
>
> I watch, and in its works of creation, nature brings forth all that moves and does not move: And thus the revolutions of the world go round and round.[5]

This creative genius is the eternal, self-existing, original essence of divine being. It is a singular, great, enlightening entirety; omnipresent, perfect, silent, and pure. It is like an all-encompassing mirror from which the mountains and rivers of the earth, sky, sun, moon, and stars are projected like reflected images.

The moment we turn our sight away from the external and meditatively look within, we realize that this one mind is our true divine self and that separate individual minds do not actually exist. The individual mind, evoked by limited, dualistic thinking, is no more than a microcosmic aspect of the cosmic mind. It is just as if we were to gaze at the sky through a straw and take our limited field of vision for the entire sky. In an old Indian parable, the predicament of individuals trapped within their narrow views is compared to that of a frog living in a well:

There once was a frog who had lived his whole life in an old well by the edge of the sea. One day a fish jumped out of the sea and fell into the well. As soon as the frog recovered from his initial shock, he asked the newcomer, "Where do you come from?"

The fish answered, "I come from the sea."

"From the sea?" repeated the frog, quite amazed. "Tell me, how big is the sea?"

"Very big," replied the fish.

The frog stretched out his foot and asked, "Is the sea this big?"

"It's much bigger!" said the fish.

The frog then took a powerful leap from one side of the well to the other. "Is it this big?"

"My friend," said the fish, "the sea is so big that your well is no comparison!"

"Now you've given yourself away, you liar!" exclaimed the frog. "Nothing can possibly be any bigger than my well!"

As long as we cover up our true self—the unlimited, transcendent mind—with all sorts of concepts and ideas, we find ourselves in a regrettable state of contracted consciousness. The result is that we are still only able to grasp a tiny portion, a small aspect, of the total reality. The unending, universals and metaphysical expanse of the mind is thus reduced to a small range of individual consciousness. A state of contracted consciousness prevents our awareness of the universality of the mind, thus leaving us to eke out a pitiful existence in the dark shadow of *maya* (the illusion of an external phenomenal world).

THE MIND: THE SOURCE OF EVERYTHING

We could compare ourselves to the old beggar who lives in a run-down shack and eventually dies of hunger, never suspecting that a valuable treasure lay buried beneath his feet. Zen master Hakuin (18th century) pointedly depicts our situation in his *Chant in Praise of Zen*:

> People are in essence Buddha. Just as water is ice and there is no ice without water, there is no human being without Buddha. What a shame that people seek far and wide, not knowing what lies at hand! They are like those who stand in the midst of water, but still cry out in thirst. Born the sons of rich and noble men, yet poor and miserable, they hopelessly wander on. The darkness of misunderstanding grows deeper around them. When can they ever escape life and death?[6]

We are in our deepest essence Buddha. That is to say, we are none other than the one mind, the eternal unchanging Buddha-essence, the transcendent source of the entire cosmos. We are sons and daughters of the most high. We are the light of light that shines through the darkness as our true self and at the moment of our awakening from the dream of an imaginary, multitudinous world ascends through the emptiness like the sun and illuminates the whole universe with its brilliance. But most of us are not able to perceive the state of our original enlightened being because we only accept as mind that which thinks, feels, and perceives. Some even think that the mind is simply an effect of brain activity inside the bony shell of their skulls or, more specifically, the result of the biochemical processes of brain cells. In truth, the relationship is just the opposite. The mind is not the effect, but rather the cause of all being and therefore also of brain activity.

This cosmic mind is the universal ground underlying all we experience. It is the cosmic focus of consciousness in its totality. It is the unchanging divine essence and the creator of all things. For if the entire universe exists "of him, through him, and to him" (Romans 11:36), its essential nature must be silent, pure, and empty. Regardless of how much movement occurs within it, it remains forever unmoved. Nothing is able to tarnish nor lessen its everlasting brilliance.

That is why the Chinese Zen master Huang-po (9th century) said:

> This pure mind, the source of everything, shines forever and on all with the brilliance of its own perfection. Our original Buddha-nature is, in highest truth, devoid of any atom of objectivity.
>
> It is void, omnipresent, silent, pure; it is glorious and mysterious peaceful joy—and that is all. Enter deeply into it by awakening to it yourself.[7]

As long as we are still blinded by our ignorance, we are unable to realize the spiritual magnificence of our true being. We are caught in *maya*, the realm of illusory phenomena. In our identification with the fictitious external phenomenal world, we are no longer able to see through the deception and recall our original condition. The deception is the real cause for the ignorance in which individuals think of themselves as separate beings, as corporeal, independent persons. This ignorance leads to attachment, which strengthens ego-consciousness, thus chaining us to the cycle of birth and death. In truth, self-sufficient individuals exist no more than the external world in which they believe themselves to live.

CHAPTER TWO

The Depersonification of the Personality

THE TEACHING OF THE SKANDHAS

I f we were to subject what we generally regard as our human personality to an exact philosophical examination, we would discover that this "personality" is merely a process of spiritual and physical phenomena that actually has no more substance than a dream or a bubble on the surface of the ocean.

According to Buddhist interpretation, human beings in their physical-psychical manifestation are made up of a constantly changing combination of individual existence factors, which in functional interdependence emerge and then fade away to make room for new factors to follow. These existence factors can be divided into five groups, referred to as *skandhas*, which are listed below in order of decreasing density and substantiality:

corporeality (*rupa-skandha*)
sensation (*vedana-skandha*)
perception (*samjna-skandha*)
mental formations (*samskara-skandha*)
consciousness (*vijnana-skandha*)

The *skandhas* should not be viewed singly or collectively as making up a self-sufficient, independent self; nor should consciousness, which in its purest form comes closest to the concept of the soul, be viewed in this way.

In truth, existence factors possess no reality at all and only have a momentary, quickly subsiding presence. The singular moments of all processes of spiritual and physical life change constantly and so quickly that we do not perceive the change. The only thing that exists is a chain of momentary existences and combinations thereof. Both the individual and the existence factors, which belong to the individual's experienced phenomenal world, last but an instant. At the next moment, nothing remains of that which just came into existence.

Sensations, perceptions, and mental formations merely make up the various appearances taken on by these uninterrupted, successive, single instants of consciousness, which flare up at every moment with unimaginable speed just to disappear in the same instant forever. Our identification with these functionally interdependent fleeting moments of consciousness gives rise to the delusion of a separate personality.

Regarding the "nonpersonality" and the "emptiness" of the *skandha* processes, which are in perpetual motion, Buddha says:

> Supposing a man views the many bubbles in the waters of the Ganges. He observes and examines them closely. Afterwards, they will appear to him empty, unreal, and without substance. In the same manner, a monk views all corporeality, all sensations, perceptions, mental formations, and all consciousness, whether of the past, present, or future, inherent or extraneous, coarse or fine, common or noble, far or near, and sees them as empty, void, and unreal. And so he says to himself: "That is not mine, I am not that, that is not my self."[8]

Once we recognize that the existence factors which create the illusion of personality are really not our true self, we no longer need fear their death! On the contrary, the collapse of the *skandhas* would signify the ascent of the inner light for those free of all identification. Concerning this, Zen master Huang-po says :

If an ordinary man, when he is about to die, could only see the five (existence groups) as void; that they do not constitute an "I"; the real mind as formless and neither coming nor going; his nature as something neither commencing at birth nor perishing at his death, but as whole and motionless in its very depths; his mind and environmental objects as one, he would receive enlightenment in a flash.

He would no longer be entangled by the myriad world; he would be a world-transcendor. He would be without the faintest tendency toward rebirth. He would just be himself, oblivious of conceptual thought and one with the absolute. He would have attained the state of unconditioned being.[9]

THE TEACHING OF ANATMAN

In view of the gross misinterpretation of the *skandha* doctrine, which belongs to the foundation of all schools of Buddhism, we should note that Buddha never taught that there was not a self apart from the *skandhas*. Instead, he taught that a self, in the sense of a permanent, death-defying, reincarnating "I," was not to be found among the existence factors. Of all Buddha's teachings, that of the "non-I," the *anatman*, is the most misunderstood.

Buddha's *anatman* doctrine is really leveled against the illusion of personality that propels people narcissisticaly toward a kind of self-shackling, in which they understand their "self" to be a separate, self-contained ego. Buddha's intention was to show the way to an experience of self that is not egotistically-egocentrically bound, but rather is realized through first detaching from itself in a state devoid of "ego-delusion." For as long as individuals live under the impression that their self exists apart from other selves, their true eternal self will remain concealed under this delusion.

Buddha rejected the equation of the true self with the ego-delusion evoked by identification with the *skandhas*. Due to the confusion of the universal foundation of human consciousness with illusory ego-consciousness bred out of ignorance, Buddha felt compelled to substitute for the term *atman* (self), the term *anatman* (nonself), meaning non-ego.

11

It would be equally wrong to compare the idea of *atman*, as used in the Upanishads, to ego-delusion. Buddhist scholar Daisetz Taitaro Suzuki explains:

> To say there is no *atman*—that is not enough. We must go one step further and say there is an *atman*; however, that this *atman* does not exist on the plane of the relative, but on that of the absolute.[10]

To equate the the denial of an illusory and limited self with the denial of the eternal in humankind would be a gross misunderstanding of Buddha's message. Buddhist authors who likewise write that nothing beyond the *skandhas* outlasts death teach what Buddha never taught. If we really want to grasp what Buddha meant by the pronouncement of his *anatman* doctrine, we must leave all philosophical speculation far behind and turn to our inner source of knowledge, the *atman* itself. This is where the inexpressible mystery will unveil itself to us, where that which is beyond all designation of being or nonbeing manifests itself as our true nature. The *Katha Upanishad* it says:

> No word nor thought can reach him,
> No eye can see him.
> How else can he be reached
> Unless you realize: He is?[11]

And Chinese Zen master Huang-po says:

> Our original Buddha-nature is, in highest truth, devoid of any atom of objectivity. It is void, omnipresent, silent, pure; it is glorious and mysterious peaceful joy— and that is all. Enter deeply into it by awaking to it yourself. That which is before you is it, in all its fullness, utterly complete. There is naught beside.[12]

Even though Buddha taught that there was no self-sufficient, separate, individual self, he still left the self intact—but with a difference! He lifted it out of the bounds of duality into the unlimited vastness of original being, beyond space and time.

As long as we continue to ask ourselves whether or not we possess a certain spirit, self, or soul, we are on the wrong track with questioning that has its roots in discriminating, dualistic thinking. We should not focus on having a spirit or self, but rather on being

12

the indivisible reality of the one mind. This inexpressible reality, which lies beyond all human concepts, is the unborn, eternal, unchanging self, the foundation of all we experience. In ancient Buddhism, it is Buddha's words that most clearly attest to this unborn true self:

There is, monks, that which is unborn, undeveloped, unmade, unformed. If this were not so, there would be no escaping from the world of the born, the developed, the made, the formed.[13]

We know that our body had a beginning and is destined one day to perish. Yet this has no effect on our true self, which is unbounded and unlimited, and thus untouched by changes that occur in the phenomenal world to which the body and all physical things belong. The *Katha Upanishad* says:

This realized self is not born,
Nor does it ever die.
It comes from nowhere and is nobody.
Unborn, eternal, imperishable, original,
It is not killed, though the body be destroyed.[14]

The following words of Meister Eckhart (14th century) read almost like commentary on the above passage:

Therefore I am my own cause according to my essence, which is eternal, and not according to my becoming, which is temporal. Therefore I am unborn, and according to my unborn mode I can never die. According to my unborn mode I have eternally been, am now and shall eternally remain. That which I am by virtue of birth must die and perish, for it is mortal, and so must perish with time.[15]

In deep sleep we are unaware of our being as "I am." Nonetheless, we know that we have not ceased being. The self of this morning when we awoke is no different from the self of last evening when we went to sleep. Although we were not aware of its continuity during sleep, it did not cease being. This self is the eternal, self-existing original essence of divine being, which is the foundation of the three states of existence (waking, dream, and dreamless sleep). It is the being from which all things emanate and constantly change themselves, and to which they return at the end; as is written in the *Mandukya Upanishad*:

> It is the lord of all, the all-knowing,
> The inner guiding force, the womb of all things,
> The origin and end of all beings.[16]

I AM THAT I AM

The self is not dependent on nor is it supported by anything other than itself, for it has no purpose apart from itself since there is nothing else besides it. For that reason, the *Chandogya Upanishad* says:

> I am below, I am above, I am behind,
> I am before, I am to the right, I am to the left.
> I am truly all this! . . .
> He who realizes this . . . is perfectly free,
> He possesses unlimited freedom in all worlds.[17]

Everything that we in our experiential world call being only has being insofar as it exists of, through, and to the absolute being; for "of him, through him, and to him are all things" (Romans 11:36). The absolute being gets its being from itself and is thus the pure reality above being. Gregory of Nyssa (4th century), one of the ancient fathers of Christian mysticism, says:

> Nothing at all perceived by the senses or viewed by the intellect has true being except the essence above being, which is the ground of the universe, and upon which all things depend.[18]

All of our questions regarding the self and being are ultimately about our self-nature. Yet these questions can only be answered if we surpass the realm of distinction and recognize our true self as the self common to all beings. For if the same essence is the heart of selfness of every individual, then there cannot be a separate, self-sufficient individuality. Consequently, a totally separate, self-determining individuality is nothing more than an illusion stemming from the reciprocal identification of body and psyche and their numerous activities and abilities. The illusion of a psuedo-self is simply a complex grounded in ignorance that has no existence of its own. That is why Meister Eckhart says, "All creatures are nothing in themselves." And Buddhism says, "All things are emptiness [*sunyata*]."

That all things are "emptiness" does not mean that beings and their perceived world do not exist, but rather that they are only pure phenomena without reality. In other words, they are not nonexistent, but unreal. These two concepts have different basic meanings and should not be used interchangeably. It is, for example, impossible for us to imagine a round triangle, which thus is nonexistent. A mirage, on the other hand, belongs to existent things although it has absolutely no reality, which is to say it is unreal.

The Buddhist view of the emptiness of all phenomena is not nihilistic. Its purpose is to make clear that all things lack basic substantiality. All things are governed by the principle of dependent arising and therefore lack self-nature (*svabhava*). The term "dependent arising" (*pratitya-samutpada*) means that there are no final realities that are independent and cannot be traced to something else. Hence, everything we perceive in the world, including our own *skandha*-conditioned personality, is a relative phenomenon of a transitory nature.

The truth behind all phenomena can only be imparted to us through a dissolution of ourselves, or a depersonification of the personality. To experience the emptiness of all objective phenomena in the universe is simultaneously to awaken to our true self.

As long as we continue to cling to the transitory through our identification with external appearances, we will be unable to experience our true state of unlimited, universal mind. Hence, we seek the eternal in the transitory without recognizing that the original source of all being, as the sole being and foundation of all experience, is present within us at all times. This source of all life finds expression in the divine relevation of the burning bush: "I am that I am" (Exodus 3:14), as imparted to Moses on Mount Horeb.

Divine being, the eternal "I am," shines in the light of pure consciousness The final mystery of all existence is experienced as the "I am" of the absolute self of which we become aware in the depth of our own being. "You will know that 'I am' " says Christ (John 8:28). He also says, "If you do not believe that 'I am,' you will die in your sins" (John 8:24). What this means is that we will die in our separation from the divine ground of being, which is the source of all life. For *sin* means "separation."

Separation from the source is an estrangement from the true self, in which the ego behaves autonomously because it has forgotten that it comes from this true self. The ego wants to be its own master and to realize itself. However, "ego-realization" is not the same as true self-realization; it is best likened to a self-estrangement that leads to the senselessness and waywardness of a poor, world-bound existence. That is why Augustine (5th century) writes, "How poor he must be, he who is without that without which he cannot be." And Christ says, "Abide in me, and I in you, for without me you can do nothing" (John 15:4–5).

Separation from the divine original source is also a separation from life. It is the original sin that stems from our ignorance of the presence of the divine self at our center. Our liberation from the cycle of birth and death, which is at the same time a release from our attachment to the world, can hence only be achieved by a radical turning inward, by a true "conversion" (*metanoia*). When we turn within ourselves and in our innermost unbecome ourselves and all things, we will then become what we have sought, aware only of "is"—in itself.

In the search for divine being, the soul disappears from itself. For "no one shall see God without dying" (Exodus 33:20). As paradoxical as it may sound, we can only experience our true self when there is no self left to experience it. Those who relinquish everything will regain everything as the divine truth itself, which all the time lay hidden as the eternal "I am" beneath the phenomena they used to pursue.

"I am" is the eternal divine WORD that says of itself, "Before Abraham was, I am" (John 8:58). It is the truth in everything that is. It is pure being, the original source from which all life flows forth in unending profusion. It is the all in everything, and whoever realizes it experiences all of creation as "I am" and can declare with the seer at the end of the *Taittirya Upanishad*:

> How wonderful! "I am," even before the Gods were. I am the center and the source of immortality. And I shine like the sun.[19]

CHAPTER THREE

The Way to Liberation

THE CONSISTENCY OF THE SPIRITUAL WAY

The eternal divine light shines within us, far beyond all that can be grasped by our senses and abilities.

But what good is this to us when we are not receptive to the divine in our innermost self, thus becoming further entangled in the creeping snarl of our spiritual confusion? Just as filth covering a golden vessel is unable to detract from the vessel's true nature, the covering filth of ignorance is unable to touch the true eternal self lying hidden within.

"Seek, and you will find!" we are told in the Gospel (Matthew 7:7). This search, however, demands far more of us than we are generally willing to give. The search for divine truth is a search in the sense of an all-consuming longing that culminates in radical self-sacrifice to God. The consistency required in following the spiritual way will necessarily lead us away from everything that is viewed by those bound in ignorance as the highest meaning and purpose of their human existence. And thus it is written in the *Katha Upanishad*:

Fools chase after external pleasures, and fall into the

snare of death. But the wise, knowing immortality, seek not the everlasting in the things that pass away.[20]

Only those who have no more illusions about the meaning and importance of their small ego and its world can fully appreciate this statement; for nothing is important in the presence of death. Such understanding presumes a great awareness of the transitoriness of everything that is worldly and of the suffering that results from this. The greater the awareness is, the more our wish for redemption grows; this wish can become so intense that it leaves no room for any other wish. In the Indian tradition there is a parable about a disciple whose head was held underwater in the Ganges by his master. When the master asked him afterward what he had thought while underwater, the disciple could only muster the words: "Air, air!" The master then explained, "As long as your longing for God is less than your craving for air while underwater just now, you are still far away from God."

Naturally it is clear to me that the consistency demanded by the spiritual way is not at all soothing or comforting. Still, whoever comes to honest terms with the Gospels will not easily be able to make light of the following statements by Jesus:

> Strive with all your strength, to enter through the narrow gate! [Luke 13:24].

> Because narrow is the gate and difficult is the way which leads to (eternal) life, and there are few who find it [Matthew 7:14].

> Whoever will be my disciple, let him deny himself, take up his cross, and follow me [Mark 8:34].

> Follow me, and let the dead bury their dead! [Matthew 8:].

We could cite many other such statements, but let us keep to the essential point. To most people, these words of Jesus have a negative, antagonistic tone. But to a few, they are soul–stirring pronouncements that change these people's lives by causing a spiritual about-face in which they are torn loose from all that previously gave meaning and purpose to their every endeavor. In their resolve to leave everything behind and follow only the divine call,

18

such individuals raise themselves above the world of phenomena, thus becoming children of the universal being. The only thing that matters to them is the kingdom of God; everything else must be left behind. It is vital that this not be misunderstood to mean that these people come to despise such worthy things as marriage, family, and society. All these have a higher truth, and those living in the fullness of divine being know to cherish these treasures more than anyone since they have penetrated the essence of things and understand the inexpressible mystery of which these things are a sign. The difference is that these people no longer cling to these treasures or anything else, since they are free of identification. In a radical following of Christ, they leave the affairs of this world as they are and are guided only by what calls to them:

> Anyone who has not renounced everything cannot be my disciple! [Luke 14:26].

> [Therefore] follow me, and let the dead bury their dead! [Matthew 8:22].

THE CHEERFULNESS OF THE SOUL

The Gospel of Jesus Christ is a Gospel of following Christ consistently, which is incompatible with half measures. Only by diluting and downplaying the Christian truth was it possible to bring it to the level of a comfortable, church-elevating, sunken religion. Strictly speaking, following Christ comfortably is by no means following Christ.

People who believe that following the spiritual way can be likened to setting themselves up in comfortable accommodations are gravely mistaken. But it would be equally wrong if we thought that in following the spiritual way we must creep along with the pallbearer mentality often encountered in the false mysticism of suffering promoted by the church.

"Rejoice always!" (1 Thessalonians 5:16) says Paul, and Teresa of Avila (16th century) notes, "A sad saint is a sorry saint." It was to these sad saints that John Climacus (7th century) spoke:

> God does not insist or desire that we should mourn in agony of the heart; rather, it is his wish that out of love for him we should rejoice with laughter in our soul.[21]

19

"Joy" is a favorite word of the New Testament because the message that Jesus brings is a joyful revelation able to yank people out of their hopelessness.

Those who understand with their hearts something of the joy of the Gospel of Jesus Christ should no longer find it difficult to laugh. Laughter, as expression of the cheerfulness of the soul, is precisely what comes hardest to those who are still too attached to their small pseudo-self, the ego. With constant efforts to uphold a mask of earnestness as an expression of their piety, these roving caricatures of Christian sentiment are not very inspiring. Those who take their ego and its world so seriously should perhaps pause to ask themselves how it is that angels can fly. "Why can angels fly? Because they take themselves so lightly!"

That medieval mysticism likened sorrow to an inertia of the heart and considered it to be one of the root sins should make us stop and think. Those who refuse to give joy a place in their hearts by fighting off sorrow have become blind and deaf to the truth of divine being. Francis of Assisi (13th century) speaks to this:

> When God's servant attempts to preserve the inner and outer cheerfulness of the spirit, which comes from the purity of the heart, he cannot be harmed by demons, for they would say, "When God's servant remains cheerful in fortune and in misfortune, we are unable to find a door through which to enter into him and we cannot harm him." The devil's part is sorrow, but it is up to us to be forever merry and to rejoice in the Lord.[22]

The Christian sense of humor is not exactly proverbial, and it is often said that the strongest argument against the Christian religion is Christians themselves. "Cheerfulness is the final word of every teaching," Mahayana Buddhism tells us. Still many Christians hold the view that joy should be kept at bay. They consider joy to be wrong or diversionary and prefer to persist in the gloominess of church-going respectability. But it is foolish to attempt to lead a spiritual life by becoming stuck in the narrow-mindedness of a puritanical mentality. The seriousness of the spiritual way can easily lead to a lack of humor and intolerance, so that all you see is "the speck in your brother's eye, but do not consider the plank in your own eye" (Matthew 7:3).

This kind of pseudo-religious mentality becomes increasingly evident, the more the inflated ego in its pretense of respectability concerns itself with external appearances. Jesus once got into an argument with the Pharisees and scribes, and attacked their hypocritical pretense of respectability with the sharpest words:

> Woe to you, scribes and Pharisees, hypocrites! For you are like whitewashed tombs which indeed appear beautiful outwardly, but inside are full of dead men's bones and all uncleanness. Even so, you outwardly appear righteous to men, but inside you are full of hypocrisy and iniquity (Matthew 23: 27–28).

The use of such strong words unmasks the pretense of respectability—of the Pharisees and scribes of today and of all times to come-as sanctimonious hypocrisy. Jesus may have been many things, but one thing he wasn't was—respectable. He represented what he would always represent and what Bernanos called "the great fear of right-thinking people." He was great fear and trouble to those who declared at the time, "He must be gone, away with him," and continue to do so today in that they have disfigured and denigrated his teaching to the point that as an alienating, moralizing theology it is unrecognizable.

Jesus never lived up to the ideal of pseudo-religious clean living. This is evident by what we read in Matthew (11:19):

> The son of man came eating and drinking, and they say, "Look, a glutton and a drunkard, a friend of sinners."

The idea of clean living is always paired with a puritanical conscience and spiritual narrowness, and readily appears cloaked as religious earnestness. Just the same, "you will know them by their fruits" (Matthew 7:16). Where there is no joy, there can be no truth! Great joy has been proclaimed to us, so why we should be down in the dumps? At the beginning of the Gospel it says, "I bring you great joy," and at the end, "They returned to Jerusalem with great joy" (Luke 2:10, 24:52). The Christian church needs to rediscover this great joy, the same great joy that was felt by the disciples when they witnessed the resurrection of the Savior.

21

But considering that hardened rationalists as well as narrow-minded traditionalists are reluctant to let themselves be roused out of the comfort of their pseudo-religiosity, we will probably have to wait some time for great joy in the church. There is no room for joyful proclamations in a place where people speak only of transgressions and cling to religious dogmas and formulas. "Free yourselves of everything!" Zen tells us, and Jesus says, "The truth shall make you free" (John 8:32). The Tibetan lama Buton wrote in the 14th century:

> Cheerfulness of the soul is a means of realizing truth, for in order to come to this realization, the soul, which was restless and confused, must become pure and cheerful.[23]

In Jesus's words, "Blessed are the pure in heart, for they shall see God " (Matthew 5:8).

To be pure in heart, we must first empty ourselves inside, and thus free ourselves of all clinging and identification caused by ego-delusion. When we are empty inside, we are in keeping with what Jesus expressed in the oft misunderstood first beatitude of the Sermon on the Mount: "Blessed are the poor in spirit, for theirs is the kingdom of heaven" (Matthew 5:3). When we empty ourselves of all that God is not, we will be filled with the superabundance of the Godhead. We will have the fullness of life: "And the disciples were filled with joy and with the Holy Spirit" (Acts 13:52). That is why Paul says, "But the fruit of the Spirit is joy" (Galatians 5:22).

Without the message of joy, the Christian religion is incomprehensible and uncompelling. And "good news" that is not joyfully delivered is suspect in every way and contradicts itself. The early church was only successful in the world because it was a messenger of joy; this changed as the joy was lost and the church ceased to be a witness of joy. In sharp contrast to a joyless and sorrowful Christian mentality are, paradoxically, the encouraging words of Jesus himself (John 14:1, 15:11):

> Let not your heart be troubled; believe in God, believe also in me. These things I have spoken to you that my joy may be in you and that your joy may be full .

THE WORLD AS OUR REFLECTION

Whoever reads the Gospel with the eye of the heart will recognize that Jesus was anything but a wishy-washy, sanctimonious holy man.

Jesus is *Christos*, meaning he who is filled with the divine spirit. The divine spirit is the fullness of life and the joy that, through Jesus, is reflected as the hope for salvation in people with whom he comes in contact. They are finally able to breathe freely. Oppression falls away from them and joy shines forth.

Such an effect is explicable only in that Jesus not only spoke of joy, but radiated joy himself. The joy he radiated uplifted people in an atmosphere of trust and enthusiasm for God.

This enthusiasm is able to draw us out of our petty fears and worries about everyday matters and the futility of human life. We hear the words of Jesus:

> Therefore I say to you, do not worry about your life, what you will eat or what you will drink; nor about you body, what you will put on. Is not life more than food and the body more than clothing?
>
> Look at the birds of the air: they neither sow nor reap nor gather into barns; yet your heavenly Father feeds them. Are you not of more value than they?
>
> Which of you by worrying can add one cubit to his span of life?
>
> But first seek the kingdom of God, and all these things shall be yours as well.
>
> Therefore do not worry about tomorrow, for tomorrow will worry about its own things. Sufficient for the day is its own trouble [Matthew 6:25-34].

Worrying is a disease of fallen people who out of a lack of trust in God attempt to construct their own destiny. They look to the future full of fear and look to the past wistfully or with feelings of guilt. The human heart is troubled and spiritual awareness is scattered; thus individuals lose their ability to perceive the presence of divine being that is always there. Since they no longer hear the harmonious sound of the music of life, they are solely aware of "disharmony" in the world. Just like a mirror that reflects only the face that peers into it, the world we perceive reflects only our own state of mind.

23

An old Tibetan parable illustrates this well. A dog once got lost in a cave with many passages. He suddenly found himself in a big hall, surrounded by a thousand mirrors. He saw nothing but dogs wherever he looked. Frightened and distrustful, he bristled and backed away; since the dogs in the thousand mirrors did the same, he began to growl, snarl, and bare his teeth ferociously. Growing terrified at the huge number of ferocious dogs he saw all around him, he fell into a state of utter confusion. He angrily began to run in circles, which, of course, the dogs in the mirrors did as well. This caused him to run faster and faster until all at once he fell down dead. The only question remaining here is: What would have happened had the poor dog just once wagged his tail?

An Indian proverb says, "The smile that you send out will return to you." We must begin with ourselves, if we want to live to see a joyful and peaceful world; this is spiritual law. We cannot change the picture of the world. The world is only a reflection of our self, and there is little sense in finding fault with a reflection.

People who walk around as victims of anxiety, fearful and tense, need not wonder when their negative attitude, which is seen by others as dismissive, is reflected in their environment. This anxious mentality sets up all sorts of barriers and inhibitions between people, making it impossible for them to recognize the sameness of their original nature. It is fear that keeps someone from being filled with love and sympathy for others, all because the small, limited "I" is afraid of opening itself up to the boundless expanse of the one mind. This fear is the cause of distrust, jealousy, and envy; it turns the "I" into a fortress, opposing all that surrounds it.

TURNING TO THE DIVINE

The decisive step toward God consists of letting go of all worries, that is, all fears and attachments. This step requires a foundation of complete and unreserved trust. We can only release our fears in proportion to how much our trust in God has grown, deepened, and ripened into an unshakable faith. The more we abide in living faith, the more we abide in divine love. And where this is, there is no room for fear.

Christian pastors and preachers have aroused an artificially produced fear of death with their horror stories of hell, purgatory, and perpetual damnation, and in this manner have done much harm. A fear of death that is artificially generated is by no means a way to salvation. For the holy church to have created this fear of death to serve its claim to be our only hope for rescue from death is a reprehensible theological deal with death itself. The extortion of morality and conduct pleasing to the church with the threat of perpetual damnation has little to do with the proclamation of "good news" and a "gospel of love." The First Epistle of John states: (1 John 4:18).

There is no fear in love; but perfect love casts out fear.

But just as love, the manifestation of divine truth, will cast out fear, fear will also increase in proportion to a decrease in love. That is why John Climacus says, "To the same degree that love dwindles in us, fear seizes us."[24] But if we abide in love, we abide in God, for "God is love, and he who abides in love abides in God, and God in him" (1 John 4:16).

Concerning the love that God is, Isaac the Syrian (7th century) wrote:

Love is the kingdom of God of which our Lord spoke,
"The kingdom of God is within you" [Luke 17:21].
When we have attained love, we have attained God,
and our way itself becomes the aim.[25]

The aim of our spiritual striving is to live our lives utterly in divine being and for our breathing to become one with the divine breath that maintains the entire universe. There is but one way to achieve this, and that is through a voluntary self-surrender to God. To surrender means to joyfully let go of all that is external and to entrust ourselves totally to the higher truth. It is only possible for individuals to attain such a state of inner detachment, however, if in answer to their devoted longing, faith, and hope, they are endowed with divine grace. To this Meister Eckhart says:

Often I feel afraid, when I come to speak of God, at how utterly detached the soul must be to attain union with him. But no one should think this impossible: nothing is impossible for the soul that possesses God's grace. Nothing was ever easier for a man than it is for the soul that has God's grace to leave all things. One more word on this: Nothing was ever more pleasurable for a man than it is for the soul that has God's grace to leave all things.[26]

Still we should not believe that divine grace will touch us out of some blind whim, or that we need only ask for it, let alone believe that we can force it through "new age" techniques of positive thinking. If we want to partake of grace as the working of divine love, there is no other way than for us to withdraw ourselves from our own action and will, so that divine love is able to work within us. Meister Eckhart says:

> Love begins where thinking ceases. But we do not need to hanker after God's love, rather we need only to keep ourselves ready for it.[27]

To "keep ready" is the same as to be "open and empty"; we should become like empty vessels into which the fullness of divine being can be poured. For the more individuals leave themselves in their turning to God, the more God comes into them. Meister Eckhart expresses it thus:

> There are few who are truly aware of this and who are steadfast in it. It is really an equal exchange and barter: just as much as you go out of all things, just so much, neither more nor less, does God enter in with all that is his—if indeed you go right out of all that is yours. Start with that, and let it cost you all you can afford. And in that you will find true peace, and nowhere else.[28]

In becoming empty of ourselves and all things, in becoming "transparent to the point of transcendence," we are freed from the deadly self-trust that is the mark of earth-bound worldly people, who out of lack of faith are more likely to trust in themselves than in God. For people who put trust in themselves and in the world of their senses and intellect above all else, there is only one chance left for salvation, namely, that they mature with the realities of life—whether these take the form of a heavy blow of fate or some other such unresolvable problem. These people will then either turn to the divine as they become aware of their powerlessness over fate, or they will lose what remaining faith they have. But faith that has opened itself to divine being in the inmost part of

26

the heart can never be lost. "This faith is built on rock" (Matthew 7:24).

Those who abide in this faith and have become aware of the transitory nature of all worldly things and the suffering that results therefrom will come to view what the majority of us have made into the content of our living, thinking, and dealing as nothing more than a meaningless waste of time. They will no longer feel any desire to move about in meaningless activity, like a hamster in a treadmill. They have attained the insight that has enabled them to become aware of everything over which the attention of most people only skims superficially .

THE NOBLE TRUTH OF SUFFERING

Buddha possessed this insight when he pronounced the "noble truth of suffering":

Now this, monks, is the noble truth of suffering: birth is suffering, old age is suffering, sickness is suffering, death is suffering; sorrow, lamentation, pain, grief and despair are suffering; contact with unpleasant things, separation from things we love is suffering; not getting what one wishes is suffering; in short: the five *skandhas* (corporeality, sensation, perception, mental formations and consciousness) are suffering.[29]

This statement expresses the highest philosophical thought and meditative realization. Here Buddha uses terms in a way that goes far beyond the everyday meaning of the words. None of the situations listed above can be separated from life, and yet life cannot be termed happy until they are overcome.

At this point, the reader might argue that while our existence in the world is admittedly no free ride, it nonetheless has its pleasurable and happy moments. This argument should in no way be opposed—on the contrary! Indeed it is precisely the pleasurable and happy things that make life seem so enticing. Still the flip side of the coin is this: Whatever joys life grants us, none are lasting. All happiness, everything that we love, sifts through our fingers like sand. What is more, nothing we achieve can ultimately give us any real satisfaction, since without knowing it, we are actually

27

looking for something quite different. This is why Augustine says, "You have made us for yourself, O God, and restless is our heart, till it rests in you."[30]

Since nothing we achieve is able to give us any lasting satisfaction, we continue to feel inwardly dissatisfied and to set our aims ever higher. Any attempt to build up a state of lasting satisfaction based on the inconstant and meaningless pleasures of the world is bound to end up in disappointment.

We reach for what we think is gold only to find our hands holding nothing more than dry sand that disappears between our fingers. As individuals, we pursue happiness by trying everything to satisfy our wishes: if they are fulfilled, we are happy; if not, we are sad. And the fatal part is that our wishes burn like a brushfire, constantly requiring more fuel. Bodhidharma (6th century), the first patriarch of Chinese Zen Buddhism, explains:

> Men of the world, in eternal confusion, are attached everywhere to one thing or another. The wise, however, understand the truth and are not like the vulgar. Their minds abide serenely in the uncreated while the body turns about in accordance with the laws of causation.
>
> All things are empty and there is nothing desirable and to be sought after. This world where one stays too long is like a house on fire. Because the wise are thoroughly acquainted with this truth, they never get attached to anything that becomes, their thoughts are quieted, they never seek. Says the Sutra: Wherever there is seeking, there you have sufferings; when seeking ceases you are blessed. Thus we know that not to desire is verily the way to the truth. Therefore I preach to you not to seek after anything.[31]

Most of our lives we are plagued by a specific, or rather unspecific, yearning for this or that in an attempt to fulfill a brief, fleeting moment of happiness. We tend to mistake pleasure for happiness, without realizing that pleasure is a mere illusion, a shadow of happiness. Most people spend their entire lives under this delusion, constantly seeking new pleasures. But everything is transitory, and transitoriness is suffering. Accordingly, true happiness can only be found in the everlasting, in that which is independent of space or time, for the present is intangible, the past is only a thought, and the future, likewise. We are unable to hold on to any moment without its being immediately possessed by the past and turned into a memory. Augustine describes the situation with very powerful words:

> These days are nothing. They go almost sooner than they come. And since they came, they cannot be lasting. They intertwine, run into one another, and do not stop. Nothing can be called back from the past. What is future, is awaited as passing. One cannot yet have it, while it has not come. One cannot keep it, since it came. The moment's flood sweeps everything away. The torrent of things rages by.[32]

The transitory nature of everything that we perceive through our senses is one of the principal causes of our suffering. This world is transitory, and transitoriness is suffering. However, we do not suffer because the things in the world are transitory, but because we cling to transitory things. Hence we suffer not because there is something wrong with the world, but—because there is something wrong with us.

On this score, Meister Eckhart says:

> All suffering comes from love and attachment. So if I suffer on account of transitory things, then I and my heart have love and attachment for temporal things, I do not love God with all my heart and do not yet love that which God wishes me to love with him. Is it any wonder then that God permits me to be rightly afflicted with loss and sorrow?[33]

We should understand these words to mean that our liberation from suffering can only be found in detachment from all clinging. This detachment does not mean we should adopt a world-contemptuous, negative mentality. Instead it implies that we should change the way we view the world in order to gain a whole new perspective that can lead us to freedom and inner detachment from things. We can never hope to achieve true freedom from things by depriving ourselves of them, because we will not be empty as long as we still desire them. Not until we empty ourselves of all preferences and desires for things, can we release ourselves from our attachment. That alone is what really makes us free and empty, even when we possess many things.

Meister Eckhart expresses it thus:

> We ought to have as having nothing, yet possessing all things. He is without possession, who does not desire or wish to have anything of himself or of all that is outside of him.[34]

THE DECEPTIVE NATURE OF PHENOMENA

Being inwardly empty of all phenomena is the imperative precondition to the experience of our original nature. What hinders us in our ascent to the divine, what holds us down and binds us to the dimension of time and space, is not our body or external things; it is much more our unsettled desires, which entangle us in the diversity of an external world of phenomena. Our liberation from this entanglement is thus only possible by way of realizing and becoming aware of the emptiness and unreality of all phenomena, leading to our release from all identification and attachment, which still binds unknowing worldly people. Such people are like prisoners who have been locked up for ages and have become so accustomed to their chains (even growing to like them) that, in contrast to those who seek realization, they no longer yearn for freedom. For that reason Plotinus (3rd century) urges us:

> We must advance through realization into the sanctuary, penetrating into it, if we have the strength to do so, closing our eyes to the spectacle of terrestrial things. . . . Whoever would let himself be misled by the pursuit of those vain shadows, mistaking them for realities, would grasp only an image as fugitive as the fluctuating form reflected by the waters, and would resemble that foolish youth (the ravishingly beautiful Narcissus) who, wishing to grasp that image of himself (seen in a stream), according to the fable, disappeared, carried away by the current.[35]

The more we become aware of the all-embracing entirety of divine being within as well as outside our self, the less we will be able to believe in the reality and importance of our ego-deluded personality and its experienced external world. Without question, those who live solely within the illusion of their ego-bound world of thought and emotion will be tossed about in the ocean of a world of change and remain slaves to their desires, bound to the wheel of existence. And so they move on endlessly from birth to birth, possessed by the delusion of countless fantasies, the empty deception of thinking. Since their consciousness is blanketed by the clouds of ignorance, they are unable to perceive the radiant truth of their own mind and thus seek the inner in the outer, not knowing what they are looking for. But the mind, the divine light inherent in all of humanity, awaits only the eradication of ignorance so that it can shine forth like the sun after the clouds of *maya* have been driven away. "When he shines, all shines through him, the whole world shines through his light (*Mundaka Upanishad*)[36]

RADICAL LETTING GO

The experience described above will be granted to us only if we are willing to free ourselves of all that conceals the mind by letting go of all habitual patterns of behavior and models of thought, or in other words, of ourselves. For only after we have let go of ourselves, will we be able, in a state of inner detachment, to gain peace and the "fullness of divine being." Only then will we attain a detachment that is much more than just an outward gesture of release, since it effects an inner transformation and "purity of the heart," for "blessed are the pure in heart, for they shall see God" (Matthew 5:8).

Meister Eckhart gives us the following advice:

He should resign himself to begin with, and then he has abandoned all things. In truth, if a man gave up a kingdom or the whole world and did not give up self, he would have given up nothing. But if a man gives up himself, then whatever he keeps, wealth, honor or whatever it may be, still he has given up everything.

One saint [St. Hieronymus] comments on Peter's words: "See, Lord, we have left everything" [Matthew

19:27]—and all that he had left was just his net and his boat. This saint says whoever leaves a little of his own free will, he leaves not that alone, but he leaves all that worldly people can get a hold of, in fact all that they are able to desire. For he who resigns himself and his own will has left all things as truly as if they were his free possession and at his absolute disposal. For that which you don't want to desire, you have handed over and resigned for God's sake. That is why our Lord said: "Blessed are the poor in spirit" [Matthew 5:3], that is, in will. And none should doubt this, for if there were any better way our Lord would have declared it, just as he said: "If anyone would follow me, he must first deny himself" [Matthew 16:24]. It all depends on that. Observe yourself, and wherever you find yourself, leave yourself: that is the best way.[37]

Thus, "leaving yourself" brings the individual from a self-enclosed, clinging ego-consciousness to true identity in being—from egotistical want to the true unlimited condition of mind, beyond space and time. When people become free of themselves, they will simultaneously become filled the superabundance of divine being. Japanese Zen master Dogen Zenji (13th century) said:

> To truly understand yourself means to forget yourself;
> to forget yourself means—enlightenment.[38]

Ego-delusion, as we have already learned, is the source of all evils. Masters of all religions have pointed out time and again that we must become simple and unknowing because the spiritual truth can only be realized by such pure hearts. That is why Zen says, "Free yourselves of everything, but above all of yourselves!" Nothing less than radically letting go without the slightest reassurance will do. This is also what Chinese Zen master Ta-hui (12th century) meant when he said:

> At this very moment, simply take the misleading, thinking intellect, the discriminating and judgmental mind, the mind that loves life and does not like death, the mind of knowledge and opinions and intellectual understanding, the mind that yearns for tranquillity and abhors restlessness, take all that and let it go at once![39]

To let go to such a radical degree means to become free of all identification, attachment, desire, and possessions, as well as of all our cherished ideas conceived over the years about the ultimate reality. For every notion of the inconceivable divine truth we can devise is merely an empty thought.

CHAPTER FOUR

From an Imagined God to a Nameless Divinity

IT IS FOR YOUR GOOD THAT I GO AWAY

We must decide if we are willing to settle for a mere imagined God, or whether we desire to enter into a direct, immediate experience of divine being. For only when we have put a stop to all of our intellectually tempered concepts of God, self, and the world can the light of truth dawn in our hearts. Concerning this, Meister Eckhart says:

> A man should not have, or be satisfied with, an imagined God, for then, when the idea vanishes, God vanishes! Rather, one should have an essential God, who far transcends the thought of man and all creatures.[40]

We will only be able to attain a completely unburdened and clear view once we have succeeded in freeing ourselves of all our cherished concepts of God, because anything that possesses any sort of perceivable characteristic, be it even the most sacred of symbols, cannot help but become an obstacle if we remain fixed on it.

The following words of Chinese Zen master Lin-chi (9th century) express the consistency demanded by Zen, with which this rule of freeing ourselves from all concepts of God must be followed:

> Clear all obstacles from the path. . .. If you encounter Buddha, then kill Buddha! Only thus will you attain release, only thus escape the nets and become free.[41]

This sounds like blasphemy to our ears. It is as if someone were to advise a devout Christian, "If you encounter Christ, kill him." We should remember, nevertheless, that the ancient Zen masters were deeply religious Buddhists. What Lin-chi's strong words really urge us to do is to forbid ourselves in all circumstances from being taken in by an image or idea of the absolute. In the Gospel of John, Jesus tells his disciples in his farewell speech:

> I tell you the truth. It is for your good that I go away; for if I do not go away, the Helper [Holy Spirit] will not come to you [John 16:7].

Meister Eckhart gives the following commentary to this:

> This is just as if he had said: "You rejoice too much in my present form, and therefore the perfect joy of the Holy Ghost cannot be yours." So, leave all images and unite with the formless essence, for God's spiritual comfort is delicate, therefore he will not offer himself to any but to him that scorns physical comforts.[42]

Augustine comments on the same passage in the Gospel of John with the following words:

> Had Jesus not deprived our bodily eyes of his human being, our spiritual eyes would not be lovingly fixed on his divinity.[43]

Letting go of all cherished concepts of God and religious ideas will always be the unqualified prerequisite for genuine mystical experience. As Mary Magdalene encountered the resurrected Jesus in the tomb, he said to her, "Do not cling to me" (John 20:17). By this he meant that she should not cling to his external appearance.

Experience shows that letting go of a personal image of God and of religious symbols is hardest for those who have deeply egocentric personalities. Such people are afraid of losing everything and therefore cling with all their might to their small, mortal self. Upon closer investigation, it would become obvious that most people are not ultimately concerned with a living experience of divine being, but rather with preserving treasured concepts of God and engaging in indulgent religious sentiments. True mysticism has no relation to emotional zealotry or sanctimonious holiness. These belong in a category of pseudo-mysticism that counterfeits genuine mysticism. That is why Huang-po says:

> Your prostrations are in vain. Put no faith in such ceremonies. Hie from such false beliefs. Develop a mind which rests on no thing whatever.[44]

And Meister Eckhart adds:

> Indeed, if a man thinks he will get more of God by meditation, by devotion, by ecstasies, or by special infusion of grace than by fireside or in the stable—that is nothing but taking God, wrapping a cloak around his head and shoving him under a bench. For whoever seeks God in a special way gets the way and misses God, who lies hidden in it. But whoever seeks God without any special way gets him, as he is in himself.[45]

LIBERATION FROM SIGNS AND SYMBOLS

Every form of identification and attachment to the world of the senses inevitably brings on suffering. Try as we might to find one, we have no other alternative but to let go of everything. Zen tells us, "Free yourselves of everything!" which should be interpreted as radically as the words were spoken. Whatever view of the world we care to acknowledge, we have no other choice in the end but to take up this path and leave everything behind. Buddha says:

> This world will come to pass and everything that is important will fly by. Each of us must awaken from our dream; there is no time to lose. Therefore, be steadfast in your efforts!

People are generally given to fooling themselves; they search for a shortcut or a religion of consolation, while believing in a perfect world in which everything has its place. Soji Enku wrote, "We live with a concept of God that must eventually shortcircuit because it does not correspond to reality."

Huang-po says:

> There is only the one mind and not a particle of anything else on which to lay hold, for this mind is the Buddha. If you students of the way do not awake to this mind substance, you will overlay mind with conceptual thought, you will seek the Buddha outside yourselves, and you will remain attached to forms, pious practices and so on, all of which are harmful and not at all the way to supreme knowledge.[46]

Cleaving to external forms and pious practices is one of the great dangers of the spiritual way. It chains us to symbols and signs, which should only serve as guideposts for pointing out the inner way to us. The function of a symbol is to point away from itself at that which lies beyond all designation and depiction. To go above and beyond religious signs and symbols means not to reject them, but rather to aspire to what the symbols and signs point to.

As long as we live in a dualistic world, we cannot progress along the spiritual way until we rediscover the mythos, the signs and symbols of faith. But as much as they can help us, they can also be our doom if we come to a standstill by mistaking them for what lies beyond all designation and all comprehension. Huang-po warns us of this danger when he says:

> With the merest desire to attach yourselves to this or that, mental symbols are soon formed, which lead you back to undergo the various kinds of rebirth. So let your symbolic conception be that of a void, for then the wordless teaching of Zen will make itself apparent to you. Know only that you must decide to eschew all symbolizing whatever, for by this eschewal is "symbolized" the great void in which there is neither unity– or multiplicity. Then will the Buddhas of all the vast world-systems manifest themselves to you in a flash; you will recognize the hosts of squirming, wriggling sentient beings as no more than shadows! Continents

as innumerable as grains of dust will seem no more to you than a drop in the great ocean. To you, the profoundest doctrines ever heard will seem but dreams and illusions. You will recognize all minds as one and behold all things as one.[47]

By letting go of all attachment and identification, we rise above all images and concepts, all thoughts and feelings, and everything that our senses and intellect are able to grasp. Upon leaving everything far behind, we arrive at the point that precludes any possible affirmation we could try to make about the ultimately inexpressible mystery of divine being.

THE INEXPRESSIBLE DIVINE REALITY

In the introduction to my book *Lao Tse: Das heilige Buch vom Tao und der wahren Tugend* (*Lao Tse: The Sacred Book of Tao and True Virtue*), I wrote about the inexpressible nature of the absolute in the following manner: "whatever names and circumlocutions we give to the unimaginable and therefore inexpressible original ground of all being, they are still just our own limited concepts and notions of Tao, but never Tao itself. Tao is incomprehensible and indefinable; since to define means to establish boundaries, all attempts to conceptualize Tao are the same as attempting to capture the sky in a net." That is why Lao Tse (6th century B.C.) tells us at the very beginning of the first chapter of his books:

The Tao that can be spoken
is not the eternal Tao.
The name that can be named
is not the eternal name.[48]

The more contemplatives are steeped in the fullness of divine being, the less they will find language capable of communicating the inexpressible mystery of the eternal. Nothing that can be said with words can approximate the truth. This explains why the language used by those filled with divine presence seems paradoxical to us. Since it is not possible to make a positive statement about the absolute, our only other option is to express it through the use of negations.

39

Because we are unable to say what the eternal ground of being is, we are left with stating what it is not. Through negation, we eliminate everything God is not and all obstacles that obscure the unrevealed reality of the eternal. Negation forces us to overcome all human concepts and thoughts, because "all conceptual thinking is called erroneous belief." It is possible for us to become aware of our true nature only if we completely free ourselves of all prefabricated stereotypical concepts.

Christian mysticism's most important teacher of what is known as negative theology (*theologia negativa*) was Dionysius Areopagita, whom many generations have revered as the father of Christian mysticism. A Christian Neoplatonist living at the turn of the sixth century, he exercised a huge influence over the spiritual history of the Middle Ages. Dionysius saw God as the nameless; the above-all-being, purity, and goodness; the superessential darkness. We must be absorbed in silence if our mind is to "unite with the inexpressible and unknown in an inexpressible and unknown manner," according to a union that exceeds all power and ability of our thinking. The nameless, above-all-being divine essence:

> reaches beyond all beings above all that is substantial; it is a knowing wisdom, inaccessible to any rational being of knowing wisdom. In a word, *logos*, it is the WORD itself, which cannot be expressed by any human word, a nonword, nonknowing, nonbeing, nonname; in short it is everything that does not belong to anything in any way, nor is any thing; it is the ground of being of all, but is itself not a thing and not being. It is raised above all beings and in none else, for it is unceasing.[49]

Circling continuously around a sum of theological negations coincides with the process of rising above the limited realm of articulation to that of the ultimately inexpressible. And in this manner Dionysius extols the divine darkness:

> Oh darkness of silence! It would not be enough to say of you, that you glisten like pure blackness in radiant light; not enough to say of you, that your brilliance is ever constant; not enough to say of you, that you,

darkness of original cause, dazzle until bursting with the luminous power of your fullness and are more beautiful than beauty itself.[50]

THE FINGER IS NOT THE MOON

If we truly want to submerge ourselves in the ground of all being, we must sacrifice all our familiar terminology, all ideas, signs, and symbols, so that we can open ourselves up to a new way of seeing. Only then will we be able to escape the tyranny and slavery of constricting and thus limiting conceptual thought. Unless we are willing to take this step, we will remain stuck at the "finger that points to the moon," under the mistaken impression that the finger itself is the object of the finger's pointing. The *LankavataraSutra*, one of the fundamental works of Mahayana Buddhism, states:

> May every disciple take care not to cling to words, as if they were a perfect expression of the meaning; because truth is not in the letters. When a man points to something with the finger, the tip of the finger may be mistaken for the thing pointed at. In the same way the ignorant and simple-minded are like children, incapable of giving up the idea that in the finger tip of words the actual meaning is contained.[51]

In the *Sutra of the Sixth Patriarch*, Hui-neng (8th century) says:

> Those who know the meaning have gone beyond senseless words; those who have an insight into reason have transcended the letter. The teaching itself is more than words and letters, why should we seek it in these? He who attains the meaning, forgets the words; he has an insight into reason and leaves the teaching behind.
>
> It is like a man's forgetting the creel when he has the fish, or forgetting the noose when he has the hare.[52]

The following excerpt from a letter of Chinese Zen master Yuan-wu (13th century) contributes to an understanding of this:

41

It is presented right to your face, and at this moment the whole thing is handed over to you. For an intelligent fellow, one word should suffice to convince him of the truth of it, but even then error has crept in. Much more so when it is committed to paper and ink, or given up to wordy demonstration or to logical quibble, then it slips farther away from you. The great truth of Zen is possessed by everybody. Look into your own being and seek it not through others. Your own mind is above all forms; it is free and quiet and sufficient; it eternally stamps itself in your six senses and four elements. In its light all is absorbed.

Hush the dualism of subject and object, forget both, transcend the intellect, sever yourself from the understanding, and directly penetrate deep into the identity of the Buddha-mind; outside of this there are no realities. Therefore when Bodhidharma came from the West, he simply declared, "Directly pointing to one's own soul, my doctrine is unique, and not hampered by the canonical teachings; it is the absolute transmission of the one true seal." Zen has nothing to do with letters, words, or sutras. It only requests you to grasp the point directly and therein to find your peaceful abode. When the mind is disturbed, the understanding is stirred, things are recognized, notions are entertained, and prejudices grow rampant. Zen will then forever be lost in the maze.[53]

Zen is a practical teaching and not a matter of intellectual explanation. If someone were to ask me what Zen actually teaches, I would have to answer in all truth, "Zen teaches that there is nothing to teach."

Zen is the most simple, yet most difficult thing in the world. But since we try to do everything with our heads, we have cut off our access to this simplicity. Behind every answer we have found by means of conceptual thinking, a new question is raised; the closer we get to our aim, the more we distance ourselves from it. We have a tendency to pose seemingly self-evident questions and become inextricably entangled in them. As long as we rely solely on our understanding, we will have no chance of escaping this vicious circle. For that reason Zen tells us: "Leave everything behind! Throw away your colored glasses of preconceived opinions and thoughts; simply look and see things just as they are!"

Where words and signs have a practical value, we should use them, but where they fail or at all attempt to exceed their own limits, they should be stopped. It is fundamental to our spiritual way that we appreciate that words can never be more than words and symbols can never be more than symbols—nothing more. As long as we remain riveted to these things, we will be firmly caught in the cycle of birth and death and undergo untold suffering. But if we truly want to obtain liberation, we must free ourselves unreservedly from all fetters of existence. By radically freeing ourselves of everything that obstructs our clear view and by casting ourselves into the bottomless abyss of the divine void, we will obtain "the great life that gives life to all life." Dionysius Areopagita, by use of his usual language of negative theology, urges us again and again to let everything go, so that in mystical absorption we are completed by union with the Godhead:

> Leave the senses and the workings of the intellect, and all that the senses and intellect can perceive, and all that is not and is; and through unknowing reach out, so far as this is possible, towards oneness with him who is beyond all being and knowledge. In this way, through an uncompromising, absolute, and pure detachment from yourself and from all things, transcending all things and released from all, you will be led upwards towards that radiance of the divine darkness which is beyond all being.
> Entering the darkness that surpasses understanding, we shall find ourselves brought, not just to brevity of speech, but to perfect silence and unknowing.
> Emptied of all knowledge, man is joined in the highest part of himself, not with any created thing, nor with himself, nor with another, but with the one who is altogether unknowable; and, in knowing nothing, he knows in a manner that surpasses understanding.[54]

Detachment from our accustomed patterns of thought and behavior is simultaneously a spiritual liberation, as we are no longer divided against ourselves. When we win our inner freedom in this manner, we arrive at a state of spiritual tranquillity and inner peace.

When we approach things dualistically, we see things from a perspective of differentiation and opposition. But when we detach ourselves from all clinging caused by identification, we transcend all forms of dualism, including the opposition of birth and death. In his depiction of the "true men of old," Chuang Tse (4th century), who after Lao Tse was the most important exponent of Taoism, gives us a good description of the mentality that is free of the opposition of birth and death:

> True men of old knew neither to love life, nor to hate death. Admission to life was no cause for elation; withdrawal from it evoked no resistance. They came and went in tranquillity. They asked not about their beginning, nor about their end.
>
> They accepted their life and took delight in it; they forgot any fear of death and returned to their condition before life. They would never try to oppose the Tao or make the slightest attempt with human means to resist the divine.
>
> Therefore the sage enjoys that from which he can never be separated and which contains all things. He views both an early death and a long life, its beginning and its end, as good.[55]

Once we are finally freed of our "ignorance"—another name for "logical dualism"—we will realize that life and death cannot be seen as two separate things. Life is contingent upon death and death is contingent upon life. The whole puzzle and mystery of life is based on its intimate connection with death. One is contained in the other, and thus both pervade and condition each other. All that becomes presupposes that which ceases, all rising, a falling. Birth and death are but two different aspects of one and the same process, like breathing in and breathing out; each beginning can be considered an end, and each end, a beginning.

Those who speak of "eternal death" or "eternal annihilation," as if such things were really possible, demonstrate that they lack personal meditative experience. There has never been a death that was not preceded by birth, and there has never been a birth that was not followed by death. Where there is birth, there is death as well—where death, birth. Birth and death effect one another. We have no choice but to conclude that where "eternal death" prevails, there must be "eternal, or continuous birth" as well. Consequently, the idea of eternal death proves to be a meaningless and entirely untenable notion.

People handicapped by a one-sided, dualistic-intellectual point of view are only capable of seeing the instability and vicissitude of things. As a result, they are aware of the passing of time, but incapable of recognizing indestructible eternity itself. Only the mystic, who has passed through the gates of death and rebirth via the experience of enlightenment, realizes the indivisible oneness of both; thus death ceases to be horrifying. When Hui-neng (the sixth patriarch of Zen) was seventy-six, he addressed his monks:

> "Gather round me. I have decided to leave this world."
>
> This news moved all the monks to tears. "What are you crying about?" asked the master. "Are you worried for me because you think I don't know where I'm going? If I didn't know, I would be unable to leave you in this manner. What makes you cry is that you don't know where I'm going. If you did, you'd have no reason to cry since you would know that in true nature there is neither birth nor death, neither going nor coming."[56]

Those who have awakened to the true nature of the mind are beyond birth and death; the question "to be or not to be" has no meaning to them. They have no more reason to cling to life. Since they have realized the wonderful oneness of life and death, they have surpassed all duality and individual limitations. They abide in the great affirmation and fullness of life, since through their dying the "mystical death" they have experienced rebirth by awakening from the dream of the cycle of birth and death. Liberation from the dark shadows of *maya* has transformed the obscured condition of their mind into an enlightened state of

45

unlimited, transcendent mind. They have died and risen again from the dead. They are the awakened ones, the enlightened ones, who have awakened to the clear light of reality. The message of the Gospel of John is fulfilled in them: "They shall not walk in darkness, but have the light of life" (John 8:12).

CHAPTER FIVE

The Way of Active Meditation

LONGING FOR A DIRECT EXPERIENCE OF GOD

According to Christian theology, it is not possible for us during our lifetime to have direct knowledge of God. It holds that "the blessed vision of God" (*visio beatifica*) can only take place after death.

Actually, individuals in their longing for the divine seek not external religious doctrine in the form of ecclesiastical dogmas, but rather the experience of truth. Reliance on belief and a religious creed will not satisfy those who desire a true experience of being. They long much more for their own religious experience, to be touched and moved by the divine.

In contrast to the dogmatic mentality of Christian theology, which rejects such realization of God, are the statements of enlightened mystics the world over, throughout time. Simeon the Younger (11th century), one of the most important Christian mystics, speaks for many of them:

> They lie, those who say that today there is no one who knows he has seen God, and that no one ever has

except the apostles. And even those, they say, did not clearly see God, and they teach that no one can know or see him.[57]

The denial of the possibility of direct knowledge of God, heard time and again throughout the history of Christian theology, is not to be found among the mystics. Whoever seeks the reality of being must aspire to a direct experience of God in order to reach ever newer and higher dimensions of truth. Christian theology relegates this truth to an experience of the hereafter. However, the mystics who have awakened to the essence of this religion know that the ultimate truth has nothing to do with a hereafter. The reality of divine being which underlies everything we experience does not belong to a realm inaccessible to human experience nor to a future heavenly world; rather, the divine self is present at all times in all beings.

It is the divine self to which Paul refers when he says, "It is no longer I who live, but Christ lives in me" (Galatians 2:20). Origen (4th century), one of the fathers of Christian mysticism, takes note of this statement of the apostle Paul in his commentary on the Gospel of Luke:

> For what good does it do you that Christ once appeared in the flesh, if he has not appeared in your soul as well? We pray for his coming to take place in us each day, so that we can say, "It is no longer I who live, but Christ lives in me." And if Christ lived in Paul and not in me, of what good is it to me?[58]

THE MYSTERY BEYOND THE SCRIPTURES

"You have made us for yourself, O God, and restless is our heart, till it rests in you," proclaims Augustine in his *Confessions*. This restlessness has driven humanity since the first budding of human consciousness in the course of the evolution of life. We will have no inner peace until the shining radiance of divine reality, the source and purpose of all life, reveals itself to us through our awakening from the dream of a imaginary, multitudinous world.

As long as we continue to lose ourselves in all matter of philosophical reasoning, theological sophistry, and biblical explanations in our search for the truth, we remain caught in the net of conceptual thought. Origen says:

> One must understand the divine scriptures intellectual-
> ly and spiritually, for material knowledge that refers
> only to historical facts is not true. When you attempt
> to draw divine meaning from the face of the text, it
> will find no reason to show itself and will return to its
> secret dwelling place, which is the only way it may be
> seen.[59]

In the words of the mystic poet Angelus Silesius (17th century):

> Scripture is scripture, nothing more
> My comfort is reality,
> And that God speaks in me
> The word of eternity.[60]

With all due respect to the sacred writings of humanity and the words of great masters, what really matters to the enlightened mystic is the secret of the unwritten, the mystery beyond the scriptures. Expression of what has been experienced by those who have awakened to the clear light of reality far exceeds the capacity of human words. "What no eye has seen, nor ear heard, nor the heart of man conceived, what God has prepared for those who love him" (1 Corinthians 2:9), lies wholly outside the faculty of intellectual understanding. Huang-po speaks of an understanding beyond thought:

> Full understanding can come to you only through an
> inexpressible mystery. The approach to it is called the
> gateway of the stillness beyond all activity. If you wish
> to understand, know that a sudden comprehension
> comes when the mind has been purged of all the clut-
> ter of conceptual and discriminatory thought-activity.
> Those who seek the truth by means of intellect and
> learning only get further and further away from it.[61]

We should be careful not to misinterpret Huang-po's words to mean that we should quit thinking altogether. There exists not the slightest need to suppress our intellectual facilities or to stop the free flow of our thoughts through the faculty of logical thinking. We need only become aware of the limitations of all conceptual thought.

49

We would be fatally mistaken to believe, as do many Western exponents of Zen today, that we must deny our intellect. Many are of the opinion that once the "evil intellect" is suppressed, the ardently desired nirvana will automatically reveal itself. It cannot be stressed enough that this belief has not the least to do with the true practice of Zen.

The point is not to suppress thought, but rather to surpass it. And only those who have reached the limits of thought in their spiritual struggle will be able to do this and risk leaping into the great void, the vast original ground of divine being.

If we rid ourselves of conceptual thought in this manner, our true self will reveal itself in all its glory and we will have come home to the source of all being.

THE PRAYER OF SILENCE

The incessant rising and falling flow of thoughts is a part of human nature. One thought follows another, breaking off and moving around within its self-made boundaries. As a result of the restless nature of thinking—brought on by ripples or impressions on the surface of the consciousness—we are no longer aware of the omnipresent reality within us that transcends space and time. "Do you not know that you are the temple of God?" asks Paul (1 Corinthians 3:16). But asking ourselves this question does us little good when our consciousness is crammed with the assorted junk of conceptual thought. The deafening din of all sorts of imaginings, wishes, and fears drowns out the divine word that speaks to itself in the ground of the soul, the "temple of the Holy Spirit." This is the profound meaning of what is referred to in the New Testament as the "clearing of the temple." In his sermon on Matthew 21:12, Meister Eckhart says:

> We read in the holy gospel that our Lord went into the temple and cast out those that bought and sold.
>
> His intention was none other than to have the temple cleared, just as if he had said: I have a right to this temple and I want it to myself to be lord therein.
>
> What is the meaning of this? This temple, in which God would rule with authority, according to his will, is man's soul, which he made exactly like himself. For

this reason God wants this temple cleared, that he may be there all alone.

Observe that there was no one there but Jesus when he began to speak in the temple. . . . If anyone else would speak in the temple (which is the soul) but Jesus, Jesus is silent, for she (the soul) has strange guests. But if Jesus is to speak in the soul, she must be all alone, and she has to be quiet herself to hear what he says.

And that Jesus may come into us and clear out and cast away all, so help us God! Amen.[62]

The soul itself must keep silent if it is to hear the divine word that speaks to itself in the ground of the soul, just as the prophet says, "I will keep quiet and hear what the Lord God speaks within me." Keeping quiet and listening to what God speaks in the innermost of the heart finds expression in the account of the *Last Supper* found in the Gospel of John. Of John it says (John 13:23),

Now there was leaning on Jesus' bosom one of his disciples, whom Jesus loved.

This statement discloses far more than incidental and irrelevant information about the seating arrangement of the disciples. It is a figurative expression of great symbolic depth. It is important to note that biblical accounts of this nature are never pure documentation; instead they speak in pictures, using signs and symbols to declare truths which otherwise would be difficult or impossible to express.

The words "leaning on Jesus' bosom" and "whom Jesus loved" indicate the greatest possible spiritual communion between Christ and the disciples, between God and man. Above all else, leaning on Jesus' bosom means hearing the divine WORD, the unborn divine reality at the ground of our being that speaks itself in the innermost kingdom of the heart. It is hearkening to the interminable divine deep, hearkening and awakening to the everlasting within us.

Awareness of the divine essence as our innermost true self first requires absolute silence and release of all that God is not. It implies no less than turning away from the external toward what lies hidden within (*en krypto*). It is a turn from the external, or

51

realm of opposition, to the internal—the all-embracing totality of divine being. It is the way of meditation beyond objectivity, the way of inner silence before God.

Remaining quiet before God is a "prayer of silence" through which we listen to that which secretly speaks to us in the "inner room of the heart." This prayer is the same as what is meant by Jesus' urging: "When you pray, go into your room to your Father who is in the secret place" (Matthhew 6:6).

What is hidden deep in our innermost being lies in silence and stillness, and in the silence of the deep springs the eternal, inexhaustible, original source of all being. Countless words trouble the soul; where words fall silent, the everlasting begins. Keeping inwardly silent before God is the implicit precondition for perceiving the everlasting within us. If God is to speak, then all thinking, imagining, and supposing must stay quiet. All faculties must remain silent and prepare a place of inner stillness for God to speak in us.

THE PITFALL OF THE DEAD VOID

Total inner silence is different from a temporary interruption of thinking. As we have already discovered in this chapter, many who practice meditation, specifically Zen meditation (za-zen), believe that the ultimate aim of their practice is to stop their thoughts and suppress their minds. However, this kind of exercise is false practice and has no connection to true Zen meditation as nurtured by the ancient Chinese Zen masters. As early as the 17th century, Chinese Zen master Po-shan said:

> Some people begin to stop their thoughts, suppress their minds, and dissolve all things into the void. As soon as diversionary thoughts surface, they are chased off. Even the weakest thought impulses are immediately suppressed.
>
> This kind of practice and understanding represents the greatest trap into which heretics can fall: the pitfall of the dead void. Such people are the living dead. They become dull, indifferent, unfeeling, and lethargic. They are like simple-minded thieves who plug their ears while trying to steal a bell.[63]

Many people who meditate are fooled into thinking that the "pitfall of the dead void" is the achievement of a higher state of absorption. The outgrowth of this is that such individuals linger frequently and for prolonged periods of time in this state, without realizing that they are being mesmerized by stillness of the mind. Their spiritual awareness becomes increasingly dulled and sluggish instead of gaining in sharpness. In the end, their power of concentration will decrease to the point where awareness of the mind will be entirely lost. The most important Indian spiritual master of our century, Ramana Maharshi, who died in 1950, clearly warned against this fatal mistake:

> *Mano-laya* means the dissolving of the mind, which is a momentary stilling of consciousness. *Mano-laya* is concentration that temporarily stops the stream of consciousness. As soon as concentration ceases, impressions, both old and new, flow in as usual, and even if this lull were to last a thousand years it would never lead to that which is understood as release or freedom from birth and death. Therefore one must be on guard during practice . . . or be in danger of falling into a prolonged state of trance or dreamless deep yogic sleep (*yoga-nidra*). In such case, if the practitioner does not have a qualified teacher, he will wind up deceiving himself and falling prey to a hallucination of release. The following story illustrates this point:

> A yogi who had achieved this degree of concentration also believed that if he were able to maintain it over a long period of time, he would attain release; accordingly, he applied himself to his practice. One day before he became absorbed in deep concentration, he felt thirsty and asked his pupil to bring him some water from the Ganges. But before the pupil could return with water, the yogi was absorbed in a deep yogic sleep which persisted for several years.

> When he finally awoke from his trance, the first thing he asked for was: "Water! Water!" As long and deep as his concentration was, it had only temporarily lulled his consciousness; consequently, when his consciousness returned the top layer broke over him like floodwaters bursting a dam.

53

Most people who practice in this manner do not grasp the difference between the temporary lulling of the mind and the lasting destruction of illusory ideas.[64]

The aim of true meditation is not to achieve a state of total rest and relaxation by thoroughly emptying the mind, nor is it to forcibly stop and suppress the mind's functioning. True meditation is to become "transparent to the point of transcendence," whereby the mind matures to a state of constant awareness of the presence of the totality of divine reality that surrounds and fills us. In this experience, the opposition between samsara and nirvana dissolves. We will continue to ripen to the point where the world that appears as samsara to world-bound people of average awareness is experienced as the all-embracing totality, the fullness of divine being. "All is filled with the fullness of God!" (Ephesians 3:19).

A crystal-clear state of consciousness, free of all limitations, can be achieved neither through denial (e.g. asceticism) nor by one-sided emphasis on a specific spiritual practice, such as sitting in absorption, or za-zen. We must not stop at anything if we want to advance on the spiritual path, be it philosophical understanding, religious signs and symbols, or one-sided adherence to the dogmatism of sitting.

There are many adherents of the Japanese Soto Zen sect who view enlightenment (*satori*) as superfluous since we are all endowed with Buddha-nature. They believe it is sufficient to sit on their meditation cushions as frequently and as long as possible with flawless, bolt-upright posture and crossed legs, ignoring all pain. It is important that a damper be put on the delight taken in the simplicity and handiness of this method, for the Zen of leg and back pain has little to do with the Zen of the ancient masters. A teaching which maintains that flawless, upright posture can be equated to the realization of the mind and thus to enlightenment is not the true living Zen of the great Chinese masters, such as Hui-neng, Shen-hui, Ma-tsu, Huang-po, Lin-chi and all the others.

The great masters of Zen attributed no undue or exclusive value whatever to the practice of meditation. They were concerned with awakening direct, intuitive understanding through "direct pointing" (*chih-chih*). Their technique took the form of question and answer called *wen-ta*, *mondo* in Japanese, in which demonstration often replaced wordy explanation. For this reason Hui-

54

neng, the sixth patriarch of Zen in China (638–713), called his method "the school of sudden enlightenment."

Enlightenment is and will always be the foundation of pure, genuine Zen; those who believe Zen realization can be attained without enlightenment are sadly mistaken. They are as far off course as those who think that liberation can be achieved solely through intellectual philosophical study or the obtuse rattling off of sacred texts. On this point Chinese Zen master Ta-hui says:

> There is a form of error now prevailing among follow-ers of Zen, laymen as well as monks. Blindly following the instructions given in the sutras, where words are said to hinder the right understanding of the truth of Zen and Buddhism, they reject all verbal teachings and simply sit with eyes closed (and crossed legs), letting down their eyebrows as if they were completely dead. Only when this erroneous view is done away with, is there a chance for real advancement of Zen.[65]

Another master, Long-chen-pa, uses harsher words:

> Alas! Those people professing to meditate but sup-pressing all thought, are conceited about a conceptless state which they call a presence, or realization of enlightenment, and for this reason being stupid like cattle, turn themselves into animals by habituating themselves to this state. And if they do not, they them-selves have no chance of becoming free from samsara [the cycle of birth and death], even if they meditate on the sphere where no forms obtain. Therefore, the more conceited they grow, the more they are possessed by the demons of their own systems.[66]

ACTIVE MEDITATION

The foregoing words should not be understood to mean that the practice of sitting in absorption is of no value to Zen. The point is that dogmatic adherence to the one-sided med-itation practice of interminable cross-legged sitting is not only in discord with the spirit of Zen, but deeply opposed to it. That is why Zen master Ta-hui says:

In ancient times, people could sink into *Dhyana* [Zen meditation] while they cultivated their land, picked peaches, or were busy doing whatever. The point never was to sit around idle for long periods of time, occupied with forcefully suppressing your thoughts. Does *Dhyana* mean to stop thinking? If it did, it would be a false *Dhyana*, not the *Dhyana* of Zen.[67]

Just as it is important to balance emotions with knowledge and intuition with clear thinking, it is important to balance sitting meditation with activity. In its original form, Zen teaches us to experience the spiritual power of concentration and repose in the inner ground of being, achieved in the stillness of contemplation, while moving about in the world.

Ta-hui gives us the following advice:

You must realize that there is no end to the tumult of samsara. Therefore, precisely when you are occupied with the most turbulent of activities, you are not allowed to go sit on your meditation seat. You should employ the highest conduct that you so zealously practiced in stillness when you are caught up in the tumult of daily life. If you find that too difficult it means that you have not yet gained enough from your efforts in stillness.

If you are convinced that meditation in stillness is better than meditation in activity, you have fallen into the trap of searching for the truth by destroying external phenomena or you have mistaken the cause of your confusion. If you long for quiet and abhor whirl and clamor, it is time for you to put all your power to work. Suddenly the realization for which you strove so hard in still meditation will be granted to you in the midst of all the bustle.

The power that is granted to you subsequent to this breakthrough is thousands and millions of times stronger than all that which can be gained by still meditation on your meditation seat.[68]

There is no mistaking the meaning of the preceding statement: the practice of Zen has nothing to do with mere cross-legged sitting. Zen is neither quietism nor the calming of the consciousness. It is active meditation and thus meditation in the course of activity. We will reap the fruits of Zen when, forgetting ourselves and all things, we step outside of the domain of practice and goal-oriented will, once we leave all practice far behind us.

Meditation must embrace every moment of our lives. Every moment and everything we do, think, or say should become a living experience of divine being. This is the very thing that the following words of Meister Eckhart seek to tell us:

> A man should receive God in all things and train his mind to keep God ever present in his mind, in his aims and in his love. Note how you regard God: keep the same attitude that you have in church or in your cell, and carry it with you in the crowd and in unrest and inequality.. . . In your acts you should have an equal mind and equal faith and equal love for your God .. . .
>
> If you were equal-minded in this way, then no man could keep you from having God ever present.[69]

There is no doubt that this kind of active meditation is the surest and fastest way to arrive at a permanent experience of the all-encompassing and all-penetrating reality of divine being, our very own self-being.

Periods of still meditation are not only useful, but absolutely necessary in preparation for active meditation, which we stand little chance of being able to carry out without disciplined meditation practice. We should never forget, however, that the purpose of any practice is always to surpass it, to reach a level of being that exceeds all practice.

With good reason Zen tells us, "The way and the aim are one." We must refrain from distinguishing between the way and the aim (practice and realization), so that in the midst of things out in the world we are aware of our true being. With such awareness, that is, in experiencing our true being while out in the world, both states of consciousness—meditative consciousness and daily consciousness—coincide without difficulty. The anonymous author of *The Cloud of Unknowing*, a mystic and theologian of the 14th century, has the following to say on this point:

And there are some that be so spiritually refined by grace and so intimate with God in this grace of contemplation, that they may have it when they want in the common state of man's soul: as in sitting, walking, standing, or kneeling. And yet in this time they have full control of all their wits, physical as well as spiritual, and may use them as they please.[70]

Here meditation has become integrated with life in the world. There is no more division between the sacred and profane, between the *vita contemplativa* and *vita activa*. The whole world, everything, is sacred, which means nothing is sacred, or, in the language of Zen, there is "vast emptiness, no holiness."

MEDITATION PRACTICE

Considering all that has been said about meditation thus far, we should remember that sitting in absorption was practiced by all great Zen masters, but contrary to what has become common among a good many Zen Buddhists of today, it was not their exclusive activity.

Over the last decade meditation has become very fashionable in the West. The book markets of Europe and America have been inundated with an incredible flood of slickly promoted esoteric literature. However, critical examination of this literature quickly reveals that most of its authors lack true experience in what they presume to teach.

Those who have the fortune to practice under the guidance of a truly competent master of meditation are quick to realize that meditation cannot be taught through books. It is impossible for teachers to give generalized instructions on meditation when they do not have personal contact with their students and are ignorant of the latter's mental state and spiritual views—of this you can be absolutely certain. At every level of spiritual schooling it is possible for students to undergo unusual experiences and be confronted with tremendous mental and physical forces, causing them to fall into very serious states of confusion. Only experienced masters who have direct contact with their students can recognize these states in time and bring them under control. For this reason, meditative schooling should only take place within the confines of a close teacher-student relationship. This book will therefore forgo further instruction on the practice of meditation.

One of the greatest dangers that faces spiritual seekers takes the form of self-appointed gurus who come forward with pseudo-scientific argumentation and purport to impart the secret techniques of Eastern meditation practices. They frequently perform a kind of mass initiation for a crowd of interested people, most of whom are insufficiently prepared to begin practice, but go on to experiment with these techniques using a "do-it-yourself" approach. Many Western meditation enthusiasts have become accustomed to hurrying from one esoteric mass initiation to the next, attempting to collect as many meditation techniques as possible instead of seriously practicing a single discipline over a long period of time under the guidance of a truly competent teacher. They are anxious and tireless in their endeavors to learn and try out new spiritual practices and are incapable of sticking with a single practice for any period of time. Quantity is mistaken for quality in this case. Many are those who all too soon feel called upon to spread their half-digested learning by letting themselves be acclaimed as spiritual teachers although they have hardly begun to practice correctly and earnestly themselves.

Whoever is seriously interested in meditation should seek out a competent teacher for instruction. But beware! Few meditation teachers are really serious, least of all those who promote themselves and promise quick results. Just as it is impossible to become a piano virtuoso without years of regular practice, it is impossible to enter the true domain of meditation without regular discipline. Perseverance is the key. Later, in chapter eight, we will further discuss false gurus and their dangerous operations, so that we need not go into more detail here.

GRACE AND SURRENDER

The essential point of Zen meditation lies in detachment from all thoughts, without forcefully suppressing or restraining them. Zen speaks frequently of "being without thinking," "being free from thought," or "nonadherence to thought" (Japanese *munen muso*), the aim of which is to give expression to the unconscious working of the mind. It occurs on a spiritual as opposed to psychological level, where there are no remaining traces of conceptual, analytical thinking. This is the level at which all human activity recedes in favor of the working of the divine; it is precisely what is meant by John the Baptist's declaration, "He must increase, but I must decrease!" (John 3:30), and Meister Eckhart's statement, "God works and I come into being."

God's working cannot be forced, regardless of meditative practice. The mystical experience of being touched and filled by the divine lies beyond our control and is not producible at will. Whoever believes that they can automatically obtain the goal of their spiritual aspirations by simply employing certain meditative methods is deeply mistaken. The great mystics, the experts of the spiritual way, never fail to call our attention to this error of spiritual materialism.

The inner encounter of the divine is a gift and occurs by grace alone. Of course we can and should prepare ourselves for being filled with God by letting go of everything and becoming inwardly empty. The outcome, however, is not left up to us. The words of the Flemish mystic Jan van Ruysbroeck (14th century) attest to this :

> The lover, who is inward and righteous, him will it please God in his freedom to choose and to lift up into a superessential contemplation, in the divine light. And to it none can attain through knowledge and subtlety, neither through any exercise whatsoever. Only he with whom it pleases God to be united in his spirit, and whom it pleases him to enlighten by himself, can see God, and no one else.[71]

In the *Bhagavad-Gita*, Hinduism's sacred scripture, Lord Krishna says:

> Overflowing with love for me, the wise worship me. Those who worship me with love, who are ever devoted, I endow with surrender of the heart, through which they may come to me.
>
> By the grace of my will, I dispel the darkness of ignorance with the flaming lamp of knowledge for them alone.[72]

The more willing we are to surrender ourselves to the absolute, the more we will be endowed with grace as the working of divine being. The more it works in us, the more capable we will be of greater and more complete surrender.

Surrendering ourselves to the eternal means opening ourselves up and becoming transparent to the point of transcendence. By letting go and becoming empty we accept and thus are filled with something entirely different. Those who out of love for the eternal let go of their insignificant temporal life thereby simultaneously accept the great life beyond space and time that awaits them. The presence of what is hidden in our innermost self will then become a vital inner experience. However this experience occurs only in proportion to our responsiveness and willingness to let go of ourselves and all things. On this point, Johannes Tauler (14th century) says:

> Within, at the ground of man, God chose his place of rest; there he finds his joy. If only one did that: perceive the ground from within, and leave all things and turn to the ground! Yet no one does.
>
> And as a result, it often comes to pass that a person is warned ten times during his external activity to turn within. Still he does not.[73]

Only by radically turning within, by "dying into God," will we experience our divine essential nature. We must first renew ourselves through the baptism of mystical death before we can awaken to our true nature. They alone will experience the fullness of divine life who are willing to give up their own. This is also an important leitmotiv of Sri Aurobindo's Integral Yoga:

> . . . true, complete and utter self-surrender, merciless obliteration of the ego. Making a sacrificial altar out of your whole life brings forth the great movement of divine joy.[74]

The earnest nature of the spiritual way is in keeping with the seriousness of true meditation. True meditation is a matter of life and death; it is concerned with risking everything in life, with dying. Dying is a term often used as incitement in the Zen hall: "No sleeping allowed, dying only!" Soji Enku shouted to his students on occasion during group meditation. It comes down to staking everything on one card and taking the plunge into the bottomless abyss of divine nothing. "Whoever has not let go of every-thing, yes even of his own life, he cannot be my disciple," says Jesus (Luke 14:26). Only if we are willing to leave everything that our senses and understanding are able grasp far behind us, will the truth that lies beyond all that is variable and identifiable reveal itself to us.

As long as we are not willing to take this step, we will remain tied to our delusions of a stable world where everything has its place. This condition will persist until a painful experience of suf-fering or disappointment finally achieves its purpose of awakening a longing for liberation in us. At this moment we realize that we have have been holding on to an illusion—we can no longer be content with our lot. We must find our way to liberation. And this means as a final consequence: "Let go of everything, whatever it is, above all of yourself!" In with other words, "Die and come into being!" For

> He who clings to his life will lose it; he who cares little
> for his life in this world will keep it for eternal life
> [John 12:25].

BEYOND LIFE AND DEATH

People who are overly attached to their own life demonstrate that they are still controlled by their small "I." Believing life within the bounds of space and time to be the sole tangible reality of being, they hang on to their external "I" which they still identify at this stage with their own life. This attachment causes fear of death. As we have already learned in another chapter, the fear of death has its roots in the illusion of a mortal self that holds on with all its might to the *skandhas*, the individual factors that create the illusion of personality. Those who through the experi-ence of self-realization have discovered their immortal self and thus the unreality of the clinging, mortal "I," no longer cling to life, nor fear death. They have reached a spiritual state beyond life and death. For this reason, Japanese Zen master Uesugi-Kenshin (16th century) advises us:

> Those who cling to life will die, and those who do not
> fear death will live. It's what is inside that matters.

Look steadily within and you will discover that something lives within you that is beyond birth and death, that can neither drown in water nor burn in fire. I have obtained the realization of *samadhi* myself, and thus know what I'm talking about.[75]

Such resolute alignment with death was incorporated by Zen disciples into behavior of radical consequence. The Zen of the ancient masters was a matter of life and death, and encounters between master and student were always, as in the following example, taken most seriously:

One day Zen master Ma-tsu [8th century] lay down across a field path and stretched himself out. A monk came along with a wheelbarrow and asked him to move his legs so that he could get by. "Let lie, what lies," said Ma-tsu. "Let roll, what rolls," answered the monk, pushing the wheelbarrow over the master's legs. Later that evening when all were gathered in the great hall, Ma-tsu seized a huge ax and roared, "Let him who drove over my legs this afternoon come forward!" Without hesitation, the monk approached, bowed, and held out his neck for the master. Ma-tsu nodded approvingly and set the ax aside.[76]

The remarkable self-confidence and fearlessness the monk had attained through his Zen training demonstrated to Ma-tsu that his student's state of mind was beyond life and death. This presence realized through Zen practice can manifest itself so powerfully in certain situations that it becomes invincible. The following Japanese tale gives an especially vivid example of this:

A young monk set off to town with the task of hand-delivering an important letter. As he reached the edge of town, he came to a bridge over which he had to cross. Awaiting him at the bridge was a samurai, an expert sword fighter, who swore to challenge the first hundred men who crossed the bridge to a duel in order to prove his strength and invincibility. He had already killed ninety-nine.

The monk implored him to let him pass, explaining that the letter he carried was of utmost importance, "I promise to return and fight once I have completed my task." The samurai agreed and the young monk went on to deliver his letter.

Certain that his life was lost, the monk visited his master to say good-bye before returning to the bridge. "I must fight a great samurai," he said. "He is a master of the sword and I have never handled a weapon in my life. He will surely kill me." . . .

"You will die in the act," replied the master, "for you stand no chance of winning. Hence, you need not fear death. I'll even teach you the best way to die: raise the sword over your head, close your eyes, and wait. When you feel something cold on the top of your head, it will be death. Not until this moment should you let your arms fall. That is all." . . .

The young monk bowed to his master and proceeded to the bridge where the samurai was waiting. The latter thanked him for keeping his word and ordered him to prepare himself to fight.

The duel began. The monk did exactly what his master told him to do. He took the sword in both hands, raised it over his head, and waited without moving. The samurai was surprised by his opponent's stance, as it reflected neither fear nor uncertainty. He became suspicious and cautiously approached him. The young monk remained perfectly calm, solely focused on the top of his head.

The samurai thought to himself, "This man must be very strong; he had the courage to return and fight me. He's sure to be no novice."

The monk, still absorbed, paid no attention to his challenger's pacing back and forth. The latter slowly became fearful. "He must no doubt be a very great warrior," he thought, "for only a great master of the sword would take such an aggressive stance from the very beginning. And this one even closes his eyes!"

The young monk continued to wait for the cold feeling on the top of his head. Meanwhile, the samurai was totally perplexed. He no longer dared to attack, certain of being sliced in two if he made the slightest movement. The monk, on the other hand, had completely forgotten the samurai in his absorption with properly carrying out the advice of his master and dying with dignity. Finally, he was called back to reality by the sound of the samurai's whining:

"Please do not kill me; have pity on me. I thought I was the king of the sword, but never in my life have I met a master as great as you! I beg of you, take me on as your student and teach me the true way of the sword." . . . [77]

Swordsmanship based solely on technical skill is not in keeping with the spirit of Zen and will fail miserably when confronted with the presence of one who is beyond life and death. True masters of the sword are not those who defeat others in battle, but rather those who have defeated themselves. Take for example the following incident:

The famous sword master Tajima-no-Kami once came upon an old man whose extraordinary presence immediately betrayed him to be a great sword master. The famous master spoke to the old man and asked him what type of sword fighting he practiced. When the old man replied that he knew nothing of sword fighting, Tajima-no-Kami retorted that he clearly saw he was facing a great sword master, so would he please cut the teasing. The old man then explained that he had begun to practice Zen early on and had since attained a state of mind beyond life and death. "That's it!" cried the master; "The secret of sword fighting lies precisely in being free from all thoughts of life and death." And so it was that on the spot he pronounced the old man to be a master of the sword. [78]

Only when consciousness that distinguishes between life and death ceases have we attained the state of mind that leads to invincibility. As long as we fear death while holding on to the illusion of an independent, self-sufficient, clinging "I," we are still too intensely focused on our own survival to be capable of winning a fight.

Those who are beyond all thoughts of life and death are far

more than a match for others who are not. The reason why is that they are able to devote themselves entirely and with undivided attention to what they are doing at the moment. They are not distracted by thoughts of victory or defeat, gain or loss. Nothing separates them from their deeds that could interfere with the spontaneous flow of their action. Theirs is the all-embracing awareness of multidimensional consciousness, which cannot be limited by willfully directed concentration. Consciously directed concentration is unable to grasp a situation entirely because it only focuses on single fragments of the whole.

To obtain such an all-embracing, multidimensional awareness of being, we must break through the boundaries of consciousness limited by nonrealization, through the death of self. However, since no single self exists in opposition to other apparently existent selves, the death of self can only mean the death of all identification and attachment caused by ego-delusion.

AT THE MOMENT OF DEATH

Without the eradication, the death, of greedy attachment to the illusory concept of "I," we will remain chained to samsara, the cycle of birth and death. This cycle rotates under the inexorable law of karma, namely, the retribution for all deeds performed in the world of external phenomena. Karma and rebirth are inextricably intertwined with ego-delusion, for as long as we remain "egocentric" as a result of ignorance of our true essential nature, we will take for reality the imaginary multitudinous world projected on the surface of our consciousness. We thus commit all conceivable deeds out of greed, anger, and spiritual blindness and further entangle ourselves in the growing confusion of identification caused by our attachment. There is no escape save through the experience of mystical death, the radical obliteration of ego-delusion.

Those who do not partake of the experience of mystical death but who truly strive for the truth of divine being in this lifetime will move closer to it from incarnation to incarnation. Eventually, and if it is at the moment of the biological death of the body at the end of its life course, the shining brilliance of the one mind will be revealed to them too. Our state of mind at the moment of death is therefore of critical importance.

Our last thoughts prior to death, and the state of mind in which we die are ultimately decisive in determining what happens to us in *bardo*, the intervening state between death and rebirth, and beyond, in rebirth. If our state of consciousness in the last moments of our temporal existence is full of spiritual clarity, inner detachment, and trust in God's love, we will not have led a meaningless life. Those who trust in God and believe in his boundless love will be led by death to glory and the inexpressible and inconceivable mystery of divine love. On the other hand, if we find ourselves in our final moments in a state of spiritual confusion, fear, and helplessness caused by attachment, resistance, and spiritual blindness, we will not have realized anything along our spiritual way. Those who die in a state of ignorance and spiritual confusion will be helplessly swept away by the negative tendencies of their consciousness.

Lack of insight into self-created psychological processes is what prevents individuals from recognizing that inner driving forces, emotions, and repressed complexes can one day rise up out of the subconscious and work against them. Only an increase in spiritual awareness and in being able to see through the deceptive nature of the ego—and above all, a spiritual disposition of absolute faith and total surrender to the divine—can extinguish the subconscious and spiritually harmful processes and turn the process of dying into an act of liberation. If in our final hours we commend ourselves entirely into God's hands, just as Jesus Christ did when he said on the cross, "Father, I commend my spirit into your hands" (Luke 23:46), the divine light will mysteriously and wonderfully dawn out of the depth of the darkness of death and seize us. We will be absorbed into the pure light of God. We will dissolve into the light of eternity.

It all comes down to one thing: unqualified trust in God. It is trusting that an endless horizon will open itself up to us in death, that we will not die into nothingness but instead into the glory of divine being, and that God's secret for those who completely surrender and relinquish themselves to him contains revelations impossible to imagine. "Eye has not seen, nor ear heard, nor have entered into the heart of man the things which God has prepared for those who love him" (1 Corinthians 2:9). What a wonderful promise! It releases us from the narrow bounds of the perceptive ability of our senses and the power of our imagination into the limitless expanse of God's eternity.

It is entirely up to us. We can be adequately prepared to transform the process of dying into an act of liberation, or we can
allow ourselves, by being unprepared, to be dominated by the
undesirable proclivities arising at the time of death, which are then
too powerful to control.

The German mystic Jakob Böhme (17th century) describes the
situation with words that are highly reminiscent of the teaching of
the *Tibetan Book of the Dead*:

> Nothing is closer to you than heaven, paradise and
> hell: to which you are closest at this moment is the one
> towards which you are inclined and strive. You stand
> in both doorways and have both births in you.[79]

We will be transformed into what we desire; this is the karmic
law of cause and effect. In the *Bhagavad-Gita*, Lord Krishna
therefore says:

> At the hour of death, when a man leaves his body,
> he must depart with his consciousness absorbed in me.
> Then he will be united with me. Be certain of that.
> Whatever a man remembers at the last, when he is
> leaving his body, will be realized by him in the here-
> after; because that will be what his mind has most
> constantly dwelt on, during this life.[80]

We will become whatever our attention is focused on during
our last moments. The long-gone thoughts of our previous existence determined our present birth, and the thoughts of our present existence will determine that of our future. Nevertheless,
beyond all thoughts shines the radiant light of the one mind with
undiminishing clarity, and nothing whatsoever can detract from
its endless brilliance. An ancient Tibetan text, the *Song of
Mahamudra* by Tilopa (11th century), therefore reads:

> The clouds that wander across the heavens do not
> take root anywhere; they have no home, no more
> than the discriminating thoughts that move across the
> mind .. . . Forms and colors originate in space, but
> space itself is neither black nor white. All things origi-
> nate from the mind, but the mind itself remains
> untouched by virtues and vices.

The darkness of millennia cannot darken the radiant sun; endless aeons of samsara cannot lessen the radiant light of the mind.[81]

The eternal radiant light of the one mind is our original face before birth. It is our real immortal self. It is unaffected by the various phenomena of a temporal existence and by the manifold forms of existence in higher and lower regions. The ignorant ego, crazily racing about, is no more than a shadow that at the moment of enlightenment, when the glory of the divine self shines forth, vanishes.

CHAPTER SIX

Crucifixion and Transformation

THE MISUNDERSTOOD CRUCIFIXION

In the baptism of mystical death, we resign our small ego-conscious "I" to death. With absolute trust in the presence of divine being, we lay ourselves entirely in the hands of the one who is the source of all life, for He is "the life that gives life to all life."

True following of Christ is attained through our total surrender to the divine to the point of mystical death. For only through a self-forgetting love for that which is love itself will we obtain life.

Meister Eckhart, in his commentary on "love is as strong as death" (Canticles 8:6), therefore says:

> Since love for God "is as strong as death," she also kills people in the spiritual sense and separates the soul from the body in her own fashion; this occurs if the individual totally gives in and gives up himself, does away with his "I," and thus separates himself from himself.

This occurs solely by virtue of the mighty power of love, who so sweetly knows how to kill. This dying is the pouring in of eternal life, a death only of the life of the flesh, which the individual is persistently bent on living merely for his own use.[82]

This can only be understood by those who in their longing for the divine are also willing to forgo all speculative, dogmatic thinking, for "love begins where thinking ends," in other words, love begins where thinking is surpassed. And since divine reality lies beyond the realm of intellectual understanding, another term for thinking, it is eternal and hence not subject to space or time. Those who will be united with God must therefore transcend time in the process of mystical death, in letting go of everything. Whatever is bound by space and time is changeable and thus transitory. On the other hand, the nontransitory is eternal; it is divine reality itself. Augustine expresses it thus:

> Immortality is the substance of God, because God does not contain anything changeable. There is no past [in the sense] that it no longer exists, so to speak. Nothing is future, as though it did not yet exist. There is solely: Is.[83]

When we abandon all temporal things out of love for the eternal, a humble love will show itself. This love does not make us poorer, but richer in every respect. "We will have the fullness of life" (John 8:12). The German mystic Johannes Tauler, a student of Meister Eckhart, described the way of mystical death with the following words:

> I speak to you in the truth that is God: Should you become a person according to God's will; all things in you, the cause and object of your attachment, must die off.
> The more the powers of the soul are detached and cleansed of the external, the more they are widened and expanded by growing within; the more powerful, divine, and absolute the word of God will become. One cannot attain to this except through a thorough death of self. Life cannot truly be in us, nor be granted to us;

we must first transcend it and come to it through
[mystical] death.[84]

Few are capable of such radical detachment from themselves
and all things. What most people lack is sufficient longing for a
direct experience of God, which is imperative. Such longing for
the divine far exceeds the emotional impulse born of a wish. True
spiritual longing is much more a propensity for the eternal, one
that fully grips and catapults us without calculation or guarantee
into the great adventure of the encounter with the divine. It means
that we allow ourselves to be thrown into an unknown venture
where there is no turning back. I like to call it a higher form of
courage, one that brings us to a release of all our familiar concepts
and values, whereby we no longer ask ourselves what will happen
when we let go. For as long as we keep asking ourselves where we
will land once we have let go, we will never take the first step,
holding on instead to our old habitual patterns of behavior and
models of thought.

Spiritual longing is a call to the eternal, a longing that springs
from the depths of the heart. It is the soul's call to the divine with
a willingness to give itself up and allow the higher power to take
possession of us. The stronger the longing, the greater the surrender of self.

Without this longing, we will never be capable of the all-consuming love that culminates in absolute surrender to the divine.
This absolute surrender is a total self-dissolution, or *kenosis*, as in
the example given to us by Jesus Christ, who lived his self-dissolv-
ing love to the point of crucifixion. To become like Him in consummate self-dissolution is the unqualified prerequisite to *unio*
mystica, the union with God. In detachment from ourselves and
all creation, we experience death on the cross outwardly and
inwardly, materially and spiritually. Mystical death on the cross is
the sole gateway to rebirth in the eternal light. The "great death"
is none other than the "great resurrection." And although the holy
scriptures say, "No man shall see God and live" (Exodus 33:20),
this statement should not be taken, as it is in Christian theology,
as proof of the impossibility of seeing God. These words represent
much more a calling to mystical death. This interpretation was
also advanced by Bonaventure (13th century), as he explains in his
commentary on Matthew 5:4:

It is perceived by the one alone who says, "My soul chooses mortal fear, and my bones death." And whoever loves this death can see God; for the indubitable truth is this: "No one shall see God and live." Therefore, let us die and go forth into the darkness.[85]

And Angelus Silesius urges us :

> Die, ere you die,
> So that if you should die,
> You will not die.
> Otherwise, you may be ruined.[86]

No one can undertake this mystical death for us, be it Buddha or Jesus Christ, any more than my drinking a glass of water would quench your thirst. That is why we are making a fatal mistake if we believe that Jesus died in our place on the cross at Golgotha. He did not die "in our place" on the cross, but rather "for our sake."

He did not go the way of total self-dissolution to free us without our having to do anything. His purpose was to show us how we can free ourselves. After all, in the Gospel of Matthew he says:

> Take my yoke upon you and learn from me [Matthew 11:29].

This point is crucial. It is the key to a clear understanding of the Passion of Christ.

The liberating act of absolute divine wisdom through its relevation in Jesus Christ should not be regarded as a lump sum, collective redemption. Otherwise, the following words of Jesus would make no sense:

> Whoever desires to be my disciple, let him deny himself, take up his cross, and follow me [Matthew 16:24].

We will not be justified in speaking of a true following unless we too are willing to bear the cross and let ourselves pass away. All religions teach that the individual must die the great death to realize divine reality. In breaking through the veil of *maya*, the individual ascends upward to God. He crosses the boundaries of space and time and rises above the fog of phenomena into the clear light of truth.

In surrendering his life on the cross, Jesus leads the movement of the ascent of man to God to its goal; this is where the absolute devotion of man to God, of the creatural to the divine, is perfected. He allowed the self to die for the world and resurrected it to eternal life. On the cross, the descent of God coincides with the ascent of man.

In the person of Jesus Christ and in his death on the cross, God's loving surrender of self to humanity and humanity's loving, self-forgetting surrender of self to God encounter one another and serve as a call to follow. In this, and in only this sense can the salvation of the world be accomplished through the crucifixion of Jesus Christ.

Jesus Christ did not go to his death on the cross to free us from suffering without our having to do anything. By his self-sacrifice, he did not relieve us of responsibility for ourselves and does not show us how to get around our own mystical death, but rather the way through it. He lived, suffered, and "died" as an example to us. That is why he is our way and even says so himself:

> I am the way, the truth and the life. No one comes to
> the Father except through me [John 14:6].

The key to Christ's act of liberation is found in his decision in the garden of Gethsemane. Faced with a decision, but without outside pressure, Christ chooses death. By this act of free will, through his salvational self-sacrifice, he sets an example for us to emulate (Hebrews 5:9).

> Once perfected, he became the source of eternal salva-
> tion for all who obey him [i.e., follow and imitate him].

There is no way to liberation except the way we go ourselves. Angelus Silesius therefore says:

> The Cross of Golgotha cannot deliver you from evil,
> if it is not set up within you too.[87]

The power of the cross will reveal itself to us only insofar as we too are willing to surrender ourselves. Imitation of Christ is thus not a matter of an outward profession of faith in the sense of a superficial belief, nor is it a question of intellectual understanding. It has much more to do with the necessity of a self-surrender and self-dissolution motivated by love, in accordance with the famous words of the Epistle of Paul to the Philippians (2:7–8): "He dissolved himself, humbled himself and became obedient unto death, even death on a cross."

For Christ's followers, such absolute dissolution of self is no less than a self-effected emptying of self into God. Effecting this emptiness (Sanskrit *sunyata*) means to unbecome everything that is temporal or creatural, which at the same time means to become filled with God. In Meister Eckhart's words:

> God desires you to go out of yourself (as creature) as much as if all his blessedness depended on it. My dear friend, what harm can it do to you to do God the favor of letting him be God in you?[88]

The "going out of myself (as creature)" of which Meister Eckhart speaks ultimately refers to the death of the ego. The attainment of selflessness signifies liberation and redemption.

CHURCH DOGMA

Divine wisdom, out of love for humanity, shows us Christ's sacrificial death as the way to liberation, "for God so loved the world that he gave his only begotten son" (John 3:16).

If we regard this act of divine love solely as the taking of a punishment we actually deserved, we are missing the deeper significance for humanity of Jesus' sacrificial death. Those who are unable to see more in the crucifixion than that Jesus died for our sins show that they are incapable of truly following Christ and of personal spiritual experience. A religion that is not renewed by the individual mystical experience of its believers will stiffen until it becomes a fossil of dead church dogmas. Such belief systems are in danger of obscuring the mystical truth with logical structure and rational doctrine. For rational understanding aims to command the truth, instead of serve it. The limited human intellect, with its narrow concepts and notions of the divine truth, ends up mistaking its own self-produced delusions for the eternal truth because it is no longer able to tell them apart. In one-sided adherence to acrobatic cerebral speculation, theological erudition stiffens to the point of becoming the dogma of an ecclesiastical institution.

Although toward the end of his life Thomas Aquinas confessed that everything he had written seemed like chaff to him, his followers rushed to build on his theological system and turn it into a shackle for the human spirit. As a result, his later mystical realizations were, unfortunately, neglected. All theological and philosophical systems are at risk of becoming tangled in the vines of erudite scholarship and a slavish devotion to words, both of which eventually harden into dogma.

Those who claim to be religious by clinging to such empty tenets display no religious conviction of their own, save one that they have been talked into by others. Their conviction does not involve true faith, but instead centers on a superficial and shallow belief that lacks the strength of trust in God himself. In contrast, true faith is precisely the strength of trust that enabled Jesus in the garden of Gethsemane to overcome his fear of death.

We cannot partake of a living faith through slavish devotion to words wrought from the dead letters of church dogmas. Adherence to words and concepts must be surpassed in order to arrive at a true and living faith, which is thus because it is lived; Paul says, "The just shall live by faith" (Romans 1:17). True faith is always free, unbound, and deeply rooted in the "love that is God himself" (1 John 4:16). On this point, Jakob Böhme says:

> True faith is a power of God, in unison with God. It works in God and with God. It is free and not bound to anything except righteous love, from which it gets its life power and strength. Nothing depends on human imagining. For just as God is free of all inclination, doing what he will and not having to justify it, righteous true faith in unison with God is free.[89]

A belief that fails to strike at the center of the soul has nothing to do with true religious faith. The accompanying ritual becomes a mere outward gesture, a verbal profession of belief in the sense of a formulated recapitulation of the main points of a religious dogma. This is the reason why a Christianity bogged down in externals lacks persuasive power.

The somnolent climate of such a religion of dutiful piety serves much more to foster spiritual weariness than to encourage individual searching. Because it can only offer prefabricated answers, it thoroughly prevents seekers from asking questions that are vital to them and is thus ill-suited for promoting a true spiritual life.

In our times, many sincere spiritual seekers have drifted away from the Christian church because the church has been unable to provide them with the nourishment needed for their spiritual growth. A primary reason for this is that most clerics lack the ingredient essential to awakening genuine enthusiasm for the eternal. This ingredient is none other than the enthusiasm for God that is born of mystical living and mystical experience.

The word *religion* (Latin *religere*) means "reunion with God." This reunion goes far beyond superficial, occasional thought about God. Above all, it should not be confused with the mechanical performance of rehearsed rituals and sacred chants. Angelus Silesius makes this point in a question he poses to all ritualists:

> Do you think, O poor thing,
> That your mouth's cries be
> The proper song of praise
> Of the silent divinity?[90]

We live in a time of the coming together of religions. Especially those who suffer the after-effects of technical civilization feel trapped in an all too mechanical world. Given this situation, how can we expect a clergy consisting of programmed ritualists and fossilized traditionalists to inspire true spiritual impulses? Such clergy make the situation even worse when, possessed by a narrow-minded dogmatic system, they presume to judge the statements of enlightened mystics from the limited perspective of their own constricted consciousness. Japanese religious scholar Keiji Nichitani comments on this type of theologian:

> These critics must be accused of discussing something that is utterly alien to their realm of experience and point of view and of standing opposite the literary testimony of mysticism as they would a printed musical score, from which only with difficulty could they decipher single parts whose arrangement and orchestration far exceeds their mental capacity. The monotony and inadequacy of the arguments brought forth

against mysticism reveals that their proponents lack the sensorium for mystical experience themselves.[91]

There are, of course, praiseworthy exceptions among the clergy. Hope remains that in the future a stronger mystical spirit will be felt in the churches.

In theological circles a great deal of energy is spent on discussing how to get young people enthusiastic about the church; but as long as the problem is not tackled at its roots, the energy will be wasted. Nowadays we often meet people of faith who believe in Christ but radically reject the church. It is also not uncommon to see young people—but not only the young—devoutly sitting in absorption in the church; yet as soon as the service begins, they immediately leave the building. Today people long for their own religious experience, for true mystical realization. They are no longer satisfied with outward ritual and the simple endorsement of the dogmatic doctrine that Jesus died for our sins.

The church dogma of Jesus' crucifixion "in our place" indeed serves its purpose as a means of binding spiritually immature believers to the church; nonetheless, those who hunger for divine being as nourishment for eternal life will "not be satisfied with a picture of a rice cake," as Zen phrases it. Karl Rahner once spoke these bold prophetic words:

> The pious of tomorrow will be a mystic, one who has experienced something, against which conventional religious upbringing remains only as secondary training for the religious institutional.[92]

The belief system that created such religious upbringing can today no longer hold its ground against the truth. As a "child of this world," it is not capable of proclaiming the "kingdom" that "is not of this world."

The crucial step on the pathway to the "kingdom of God" is to free yourself of all encrusted theological and philosophical notions and, concurrently, to free yourself of your own ego. The accomplishment of this release occurs through a process of inner cleansing, possible only by way of meditative practice in which all rational concepts of God are surpassed. Bonaventure says:

> The mind needs cleansing in order to attain perfect

realization. The intellect is cleansed when it disregards all impressions of sensual perception; it is further cleansed when it is free from visions too. It is entirely cleansed when it is free of philosophical reasoning.[93]

Won by means of the meditative way, the liberation from all theological and philosophical models of thinking—old as well as new—raises us above all forms of constricting conceptual thought. For after all, the point is not to replace our old way of thinking with a new way, regardless of how scientifically grounded it is, but rather to surpass both and, via the mystical way, arrive at a mystical consciousness. This way, however, leads straight through the death of the ego, beginning with the many small deaths we must die along the spiritual way until the great death occurs.

THE ABYSS OF THE DIVINE VOID

An imitation of Christ as radically interpreted as this demands complete surrender to the divine. There can be no liberation without it. It is more than just one of the necessary preconditions; it is the primary, indispensable posture.

Surrender means to give our all to the divine, to offer up everything that we are and have, and not to insist on anything, be it our own ideas, desires, habits, or whatever. Surrender to the divine means to renounce our own self-made, ego-induced boundaries and to allow the almighty substantiality of the one mind to take possession of us.

A halfhearted wish, mere thought, or empty talk about surrender will not cut it. Without a push towards a radical and total alteration of consciousness in which we entrust our lives entirely to the divine, we will remain caught in the nets of our worldly involvements. Our last remaining impulses, activities, and habits must be relinquished and offered to the divine, so that all of our old piled-up conditioning, in the form of ingrained models of thinking and patterns of behavior, can be consumed by the fire of divine truth.

The true way is surrender: absolute and unconditional surrender to divine reality. True surrender expands us; it extends our abilities; it confers on us tremendous faculties impossible for us to equal on our own.

80

We will enter an altogether new world, one which we could never have entered had we not surrendered ourselves. Yet our surrender must be so radical that it ends with the mystical death of self. In the words of Islamic mystic al-Ghazali (12th century):

> At night you must plunge,
> Into the depths of your nothing,
> Should a morning dawn for you
> In the brilliance of the highest light.[94]

The mystical death process is not an agreeable affair; for it is a dying which could possibly, depending on the nature of our attachments, turn into a formidable internal conflict.

The ego resists to the last. At this point we will find ourselves at the edge of an unfathomably deep abyss with nothing left to secure our hold. Gregory of Nyssa gives us a very vivid depiction:

> Imagine a sheer, steep crag, with a projecting edge at the top. Now imagine what a person would probably feel if he put his foot on the edge of this precipice, and, looking down into the chasm below, saw no solid footing or anything to hold on to. This is what I think the soul experiences when it goes beyond its footing in material things, in its quest for that which has no dimension and which exists from all eternity. For here there is nothing it can take hold of, neither place nor time, neither measure nor anything else; our minds cannot approach it. And thus the soul, slipping at every point from what cannot be grasped, becomes dizzy and perplexed.[95]

Zen master Hakuin's description of the process sounds much like Gregory of Nyssa's:

> If you want to arrive at true egolessness, you must once and for all let go your hold over the abyss. When you rise again afterwards, you will encounter your real ego. What does it mean to let go of your hold over the abyss? Suppose a man has lost his way and arrives at a place where no one else has ever set foot. In front of him yawns a precipitous abyss. The rugged rock on which he stands is covered with slippery moss, giving him no sure

foothold. He can neither advance nor retreat, death alone awaits him. The vine he has grasped with his left hand offers him little hope; his very life hangs by a thread. If he should suddenly let go his hold, his skinny body would be crushed to pieces, bones and all.

It is the same with the student of Zen. He will come to where his mind will feel dead, his will extinguished; vast emptiness over the abyss, no hold for hand or foot. All thoughts disappear and a cold fear spreads over him. All of a sudden he finds his mind and body wiped out of existence. This is what is known as the moment of "letting go your hold over the abyss." Great joy surges forth. This is called rebirth in the pure land, this is called seeing into your own nature.[96]

The infinite abyss of the divine void opens wide before us. We are on the verge of mystical death. The dilemma at the brink of the abyss of the divine void is called the "great doubt" in Zen Buddhism. But this is no doubt in the ordinary sense of the word. It is a special kind of doubt, a doubt without content, or to be more exact, a pure sense of doubt. It functions as a sort of spiritual barrier and brings the flow of thinking to a standstill, thereby creating great mental tension. Zen also uses the term "mass of doubt" (Chinese *It'uan*), because this state of consciousness is like a mass or load that oppresses the mind.

Hearing that great doubt always precedes enlightenment may invoke feelings of spiritual uneasiness and fear in some people. All the same, it is important to remember that nothing can bring greater happiness than the breakthrough from the delusion of a temporal, myriad world into the limitless vastness of the enlightened mind. The transition from great doubt to great enlightenment is like the explosion of a huge rock in which you were encased. Yet without the spiritual guidance of an enlightened master, very few will come to great doubt, much less to great liberation. The "great doubt" is indispensable to the "great awakening."

The ancient Zen masters said:

The greater the doubt, the greater the awakening; the smaller the doubt, the smaller the awakening. No doubt, no awakening.[97]

In facing the pivotal predicament of great doubt, we have unde-
niably given up a great portion of our creatureliness, but we do
not yet feel sustained by the divine. And so we are scared off, fear-
ing being sucked into the bottomless abyss of the void and unable
to return to life. In Huang-po's words:

> Those who hasten towards it dare not enter, fearing to
> hurtle down through the void with nothing to cling to.
> So they look to the brink and retreat. . . . They are
> afraid to empty their minds lest they may plunge into
> the void. They do not know that their own mind is the
> void.[98]

That is why Chinese Zen master Po-chan advised:

> Don't worry about whether or not you will be able to
> come to life again after mystical death; worry instead
> about whether you will be able to come to death from
> the state of "life!" The ancient masters said:

> "Bravely let go
> At the brink of the cliff.
> Hurtle yourself into the void
> With complete resolution and trust.
> Only after death do we begin to live.
> This alone is the truth!"[99]

Jesus used a grain of wheat to symbolize the indispensability of
mystical death as the inevitable prerequisite for mystical resurrection (John 12:24–25):

> Unless a grain of wheat falls into the earth and dies, it
> remains alone; but if it dies, it bears much fruit. He who
> clings to his life shall lose it; and he who has little regard
> for his life in this world shall keep it for eternal life.

We can never hope to approach mystical death without unshakable and unreserved trust in divine being. And I am not talking
here about pseudo-trust, which is a superficial, intellectualized
belief in something, but rather about trust which is the way of the
soul. This trust of the soul remains steadfast at times when faith
wavers and fails. It endures even when we have no set rationalized
belief and our intellect doubts, resists, and rejects everything.

All who seriously apply themselves to the spiritual way are familiar with periods of disappointment, darkness, and lack of faith. Yet during these times there is something that sustains us and prevails, in spite of all doubt. It is something deep inside that tells us that what we have devoted ourselves to is true, regardless of all else. This trust is not the faltering trust of beginners on the spiritual path, but a great trust that must first mature.

Once we have earnestly followed the spiritual way over a period of time, the trust of our heart will be able to survive all inner and outer attacks and all doubt. Even though this resolute trust may appear as blind trust to the doubting intellect, it is nevertheless infinitely wiser than any human, logical, reasoning intelligence.

The more consummate our trust, efforts, and surrender are, the more aligned we will be with the divine (Sanskrit *ekagrata*). Our whole life will become a prayer dedicated to the divine.

CHAPTER SEVEN

Ascent to Light

THE CAVE OF THE HEART

D ying into the dark abyss of the divine void is awakening to the reality of everlasting divine being.

In the "dark night of the mind and senses," the ego disappears and the true self is resurrected, bathed in the eternal brilliance of its true face before its birth. Total night must fall within us for the inner sun to rise. The darker it becomes, the brighter the light shines in us. This light, says the Gospel of John, "is the true light which enlightens every man who comes into this world" (John 1:9).

The voices of great enlightened mystics of all ages and cultures bear witness to this unborn "divine light that shines in the darkness" (John 1:5), including that of the most important Flemish mystic of the Middle Ages, Jan van Ruysbroeck (13th century):

> In the abyss of this darkness, in which the loving spirit has died to itself, there begin the manifestation of God and eternal life. For in this darkness there shines and is born an incomprehensible light, which is the son of God, in whom we behold eternal life.[100]

And in his Second Epistle to the Corinthians, Paul writes:

For it is God who said, "Let light shine out of the darkness," who has shone in our hearts to give the light of
the knowledge of the glory of God [2 Corinthians 4:6].

But for as long as the superficial sensuality of the external,
material world continues to wholly occupy the interest of the consciousness, and the compulsion of conceptual-analytical thinking
continues to dominate, the inner light will be covered by the veil
of *maya*. That is why Jan van Ruysbroeck tells us:

You will never ever know the truth,
If you only live exteriorly in the fetters of sensuality.
Clear knowledge originates from within,
The light that breaks the darkness, from within.[101]

Not until all external and internal compulsions—in other
words, all patterns of behavior and thought—have been eliminat-
ed will the inexpressible mystery of the "birth of God" in the
ground of the soul manifest itself. The "ground of the soul," as it
is referred to by Christian mystics, is the innermost part of man. It
is the center of our being, the point and source of all life. It is the
cave of divine darkness, the *krypta* of the heart. Within it, the
light of our true nature illuminates the whole universe like the sun
and is revealed to us through beholding the hidden—*en krypto*.
This, our "temple of the Holy Spirit" (1 Corinthians 6:19), is the
guha-hridaya, the cave of the heart of the Upanishads, in which,
as the innermost sanctum of man, the unborn light of God is concealed. The *Chandogya Upanishad* says:

The light that shines higher than the heavens and
above all worlds, beyond everything, higher than the
highest worlds, is the same light that shines in the
hearts of men.[102]

And the *Mundaka Upanishad* states:

Supreme, divine, beyond all thought,
Subtler than the subtlest he shines,
Farther than the farthest, and yet so near,
Hidden in the cave of the heart.[103]

In the infinite darkness of the cave of the heart, at the moment
of mystical death, we will take part in the ascent of the inner light.

This is the great moment of our awakening from the dream of an imaginary, manifold world.

In this breakthrough to our true being, we overstep the limitations of human existence. We witness our ascent above the dark fog of phenomena into the clear light of the truth.

The great death, as it is called in Zen, is revealed to be the great resurrection, bringing an unknown mystic to declare:

> And suddenly it is there: the light. Like the morning star, it lights up in the center of the heart and raises me up, out, and over myself.
>
> I dissolve into the endless ocean of divine light. It is a radiant white light of unearthly beauty, more brilliant than a thousand suns. It floods my entire being and lifts me up in an indescribable sublime ecstasy, in perfect oneness with him. In this light I know myself to be that which I always was, am, and will be. I am spaceless and timeless eternity, limitless being, and absolute consciousness.
>
> I am newborn—reborn, resurrected from the dead.

As paradoxical as it may seem, the decline and death of the self-clinging ego is the rising of the Godhead. In the process of transformation, what we perceive as dying is revealed to be the passage from death to life.

A BOUNDLESS LIGHT

Surpassing all that our senses and intellect are able to comprehend, we are immersed in an endless ocean of divine light. We have risen from the dead. The wall of death has been penetrated, the temple curtain has been torn away, exposing the holy of holies. As we fully trust in the divine promise, the words of Christ come true:

> He who hears my word and believes him who sent me, has eternal life [and] has passed from death into life [John 5:24].

In the secret of the cave of the heart, the light that we all seek is revealed to us. Inaccessible to the senses and intellect, it is the radiant glory of *atman*, our true self. It is the breath, the cosmic respiration and thereby the "life that gives life to all life." As "the true light which enlightens every man who comes into the world," (John 1:9), it says of itself:

> I am the light of the world. He who follows me shall not walk in darkness, but have the light of life [John 8:12].

Buddhism calls it *Amitabha*, the "boundless light," and venerates it as the Buddha of the western paradise, which is not understood as a place, but as the immanent divine reality that is always present within us. Christ called it the "kingdom of God." When asked about the kingdom of God, he responded:

> The kingdom of God does not come with signs to be observed. Nor can one say "Look, here!" or "There it is!" for behold, the kingdom of God is within you [Luke 17:20-21].

The inner kingdom of God is the eternal divine light proclaimed in the *Prologue* to the Gospel of John:

> And the light shines in the darkness, and the darkness did not comprehend it (John 1:5).
>
> The true light that enlightens every man came into the world. He was in the world, and the world was made through him, yet the world did not know him. He came to his own, and his own did not receive him. But to all who received him, he gave power to become children of God [John 1:9-12].

The light, witnessed by all great mystics everywhere throughout time and to which the Gospel of John testifies here, is more than just a symbol for the divine; it is the direct self-revelation of God. Bonaventure confirms this:

> In truth, God is light, and the nearer we come to him, the more we receive of his light.[104]

All who have awakened to the reality of being beyond time and space have experienced God as light. The experience of divine light will always be granted to those who have totally relinquished themselves out of love for the divine and are prepared to receive him. Simeon the Younger (also known as Simeon the New Theologian), doubtless the most important mystic of the Greek church, was among those prepared to receive God:

> And as I diligently sought him, I suddenly discovered that he was inside of me, and at the center of my heart he appeared like the light of the round disk of the sun.
>
> He is present within me and shines in my heart; he clothes me in undiminishing brilliance and illuminates my limbs, embracing me completely. I take my fill of his love and beauty and am pervaded by the bliss and sweetness of the Godhead. I partake of the light and the glory, and my countenance shines like that of the one who is my desire; and all my limbs become light. He and I have become one.[105]

Simeon experienced union with the divine light more than once:

> Again the light shone upon me, again I saw the light with clarity. Again it opened the heavens, again it drove away the night. Again it revealed everything. Again it led me away from all visible things belonging to the senses, tore me away from them. And he who is above all heavens again communed with my spirit, without leaving heaven.
>
> And the light raised me up above everything, and I, who was amid all things, am outside of everything; I do not know if I was outside of my body also. Now I am in truth fully there, where he is simply and solely light.[106]

Imakita Kosen, a famous Japanese Zen master of the Meiji period (19th century), gives the following description of his enlightenment experience:

> One night, the boundaries of sooner and later suddenly fell away. I entered the glorious realm of the wondrous. I found myself at the ground of the great death; no awareness of my being or the being of anything else remained. I could only feel how a presence in my body expanded itself into ten thousand worlds and how an

unending brilliant light emerged. Overjoyed, I forgot that my hands waved in the air on their own and that my feet danced.[107]

BREAKTHROUGH TO THE ULTIMATE REALITY

In the inner room of the heart, the eternal light shines as "the life that gives life to all life." This is where we, beyond all form and designation, are one with the endless mystery, dying into the fullness of divine nothing, which embraces us and unites us with itself. The one who experiences, the experience, and what is experienced are one; in the words of Meister Eckhart:

> If God is to be seen, it must be in the light that is God himself.[108]
>
> The eye with which I see God is the same eye with which God sees me: my eye and God's eye are one eye, one seeing, one knowing and one love.[109]

When divine truth is experienced, the one who has attained enlightenment can no longer say, "I have seen God," nor can this person say, "I was one with God," rather only, "I *was* God." However, owing to the extraordinary nature of this declaration, we must add the words of Meister Eckhart:

> So long as a man is not equal to this truth, he cannot understand my words, for this is a naked truth which has come direct from the heart of God.[110]

The breakthrough to the ultimate reality is not, nor will it ever be, achievable by human means. Enlightenment remains a gift of divine grace. As such, those who are utterly overpowered by this experience and struck by it to the core of their being will realize without a doubt, "I am not the cause of this experience; rather, it has seized me."

The breakthrough to the divine light always occurs unexpectedly, most often at times outside of meditation. Some may be granted the enlightenment experience quite suddenly and in an unforeseen fashion, shortly before falling asleep. Precisely at the moment when we are relaxed and let go—or, better said, when we ourselves become release—will everything be given to us. It may happen to others while reading the familiar lines of a religious text to which their spiritual eye had been closed before. Often the direct stimulus is just a sound: a bell, a birdsong; or the sight of a leaf falling from a tree, or a flower. It was a sound of a frog jumping into water as he sat by an old pond in the monastery garden that became the stimulus for Zen poet Basho's (17th century) great awakening. Hereupon, he wrote his famous haiku (Zen poem):

> The old pond—
> A frog leaps in,
> And a splash.[111]

We will be struck by enlightenment as if by lightning, and we will know: *This is it!*

Meister Eckhart confirms in *The Nobleman*:

> When a man, the soul, the spirit, sees God, he realizes
> and knows himself as knowing. That is, he knows that
> he sees and knows God.[112]

At the moment of cosmic awakening, those who are granted the grace of seeing God undergo what the unknown author of the 14th-century work *The Cloud of Unknowing* describes with the following words:

> You will see your God and your love, and being
> made spiritually one with his love, nakedly experience
> him at the sovereign point of your spirit. Here, utterly
> despoiled of self and clothed in nothing but him, you
> will experience him as he really is, in all clarity. With
> the purity of an undivided heart, far removed from all
> illusion and error, you will perceive and feel that it is
> unmistakenly he, as he really is.
> The mind which sees and experiences God as he is
> in his naked reality, is no more separate from him
> than he is from his own being, which is one in essence
> and nature.[113]

The "birth of God in the soul" becomes a living event for all who awaken at the moment of enlightenment to the birthless and deathless reality of their true self. They realize that they are unborn and immortal: eternity itself. They have returned to the origin of all being, to the inexhaustible source of all life. They know themselves to be their own cause and the cause of all things, and they may join Meister Eckhart in declaring:

> In my eternal birth all things were born, and I was the cause of myself and all things: and if I had so willed it, I would not have been, and all things would not have been. If I were not, God would not be either. I am the cause of God's being God: if I were not, then God would not be God.[114]

CHAPTER EIGHT

Encounter with the Master

THE SEARCH FOR A MASTER

When Buddha was once asked how many people he thought led meaningful lives, he scraped up a bit of dirt from the ground with his fingernail and, referring to the dust under his nail, said, "This many as compared to the weight of the world."[115]

Many of us regard this statement as a gross exaggeration. All the same, we cannot deny that most of us spend our whole lives chasing after useless worldly things, thereby wasting precious time. Many lead outwardly spiritual lives, but get so caught up in externals that the real substance of spiritual truths is unable to penetrate their hearts. In addition, some followers of the spiritual way feel all too quickly called upon to spread their half-digested truths to others and succumb to the temptation of letting themselves be celebrated as spiritual teachers. They take up the battle against other people's egos, but leave their own untouched. And others mistakenly believe that they have put a definitive end to their own ego-delusion, without realizing that their ego sneaked back in through the rear door—only this time, twice as big as before.

That sly old fox, the ego, appears as an angel of light, pretending to be holy. In this situation, the spiritual seeker's ego retains the upper hand and takes only from spiritual teaching whatever suits its purposes, while rejecting the rest. What spiritual strivers seldom realize is that the spiritual misunderstanding and the yearning for spiritual truth can exist side by side—and most of the time do.

In our times, those who embark on the spiritual way without a competent master (of which there are fewer than you might think) find themselves in the same predicament as someone lost deep in the jungle. They are helpless without the aid of an experienced guide who knows all the dangers along the way and how to avoid and overcome them. Having been satisfied with worldly ego-consciousness until now, they suddenly recognize their imprisonment in the conditional and thus transitory world and are at a turning point. Once they hear the inner call of the divine that speaks to them in the ground of the soul and feel an increasingly stronger desire to follow this call, the student in them has awakened. Still, they only truly become students when they are prepared to devote everything to this inner calling and, in answer to it, search for a master to guide them. The search for a master is the search for the meaning of life. Whoever seeks a master seeks a spiritual guide in whom the meaning of life shines through as the divine truth.

"Seek, and you will find" (Matthew 7:7), says Christ. Those who seek are already on the way, owing to the fact that because they seek, they sense much more of true life than others who do not seek. Those who seek, will find—or, better said, will be found. Finding, in this sense, does not mean the usual seeing and grasping of something. It is better compared to enabling yourself to be found as the result of total release on your part. Take, for example, the man who stood before the door to paradise, trying to enter. All night long he pushed against the door with all his might. Finally, after he had collapsed in exhaustion, the door opened toward him on its own.

If we want to pass through the gate of truth, we must let everything go and leave everything behind: everything that supports us and makes us feel secure, all religious concepts, and all patterns of behavior and models of thought; all must be left behind. The master always questions everything and with the sword of realization cuts to pieces all that the student clings to with the desperate helplessness of a drowning person. Masters will use whatever means are necessary to unhinge the ego and its deceptive world and pull the rug of pseudo-reality out from under the feet of their students. Whatever is believed by the students will be rejected by the master. Whatever they cling to will be wrenched away from them. Whatever the students become convinced of will be mocked. Whatever they think themselves to be will be exposed as illusion. Whatever they think they know will be dismissed as outright nonsense.

The first time I encountered my master, Soji Enku, who died in 1977, he asked me what I had read about Zen. With pride I replied, "Almost everything that has been published in the German language." Hardly had I finished my sentence when the master jumped up from his seat and walked through the meditation hall, clapping his hands over his head while calling out, "Did you hear that? How horrible, how dreadful!" He finally stopped in front of me, and looking at me kindly, said in a quiet tone: "Dear young friend, I would like to give you a good piece of advice—take all of your books and throw them out the window. The accumulation of philosophical knowledge has nothing to do with Zen and is directly opposed to it. Zen is a practical teaching and not a thing of intellectual explanation."

Later, as I was leaving he called after me, "Yes, yes, dear Mr. Kopp has too much in his Kopp—a pun on *koph*, the German word for head."

THE DIRECT METHOD OF THE ZEN MASTER

*Z*en is based entirely on practice and attaches no value to intellectual explanations. Never have so many books been torn up and burned as in the study of Zen, and therefore my master's behavior in the above situation was not unusual.

A real Zen master constantly endeavors to free students of intellectual rubbish. The master will never relent in attempting to lead them directly to the truth of Zen. Any method may be used—a kick, a blow with a stick, or a yell—to smash chaotic intellectual concepts and explanations to pieces. The master's aim is, with uncompromising directness, to lead students to the reality of their true nature. Chinese Zen master Shih-kung once asked his head monk the following question:

"Can you grasp empty space?" The monk replied, "Yes, master." "How then?" asked the master. The monk proceeded to stretch out his arm, and suddenly grasped at the empty space. At this the master remarked, "How can you grasp empty space in this manner?" "How else?" answered the monk. He had hardly spoken these words, when the master grabbed the monk's nose and gave it a fierce tug. The monk shrieked in pain and cried, "Ow, ow, you are hurting me terribly!" The master released his nose and said, "There is no way you can grasp empty space."[116]

If an individual, like the monk in our example, claims to have attained something, it is a sure sign of error. In actuality, there is nothing to be attained nor anything to be achieved in Zen. There is only mysterious, silent understanding and nothing more.

Everything in Zen is very simple and direct. Still, most of us are convinced that the truth is only worth the effort if it is presented as a far distant and practically unobtainable goal. "What is Zen?" a student once asked my master, Soji Enku. "The ground beneath your feet" was the answer.

There is nothing special or secret about Zen. It is found precisely in the most ordinary things of everyday life. It is always present—"at this very moment!" The entire mystery and wonder of Zen lies in drinking a glass of water or tying shoelaces. An old Zen saying runs "Miraculous deeds and acts of wonder! I draw water and fetch kindling." The wonder of such things is only evident to those of us who experience the moment. That is why Zen tells us "Seize the moment and be here now!" In other words: "See everything just as it is, and do not cling to the patterns of your dualistic and limited points of view!"

Zen is living without fetters, living in freedom, and freedom itself. Once the chains of the small clinging ego are broken, our true self, ever-present, all-encompassing, and all-pervasive, shines forth in all its glory!

Our original Buddha-nature is, from the standpoint of the highest truth, without the slightest distinction or opposition. It is ever-present, silent and pure, and manifests itself as mysterious, peaceful joy. The whole perfection of divine being is with us every moment of our lives without our being aware of it.

In the encounter between master and student, the master endeavors to help students directly experience their true being. The master's powerful manner can be hard on a student, but any gruff treatment is always tempered with good-humored kindness.

A monk asked Ma-tsu, "What is Zen?" Ma-tsu knocked him to the ground and said, "If I did not strike you to the ground, the whole country would laugh at me." Ma-tsu, already introduced in the fifth chapter, was one of the most significant and most capable Zen masters of the Tang dynasty (618–907), the golden age of Zen. His powerful teaching methods led many a student to the experience of enlightenment.

Ma-tsu's most notable disciple was Pai-chang, who later became the master of a Zen giant, Huang-po. Ma-tsu's hands-on teaching method became the trigger for Pai-chang's great awakening.

> One day Pai-chang was with his master Ma-tsu in the garden behind the house. As they saw a flock of wild geese cross the sky, Ma-tsu asked, "What is that?"
>
> "Wild geese, master."
>
> "Where are they flying?"
>
> "They have flown away, master."
>
> Ma-tsu suddenly grabbed the end of Pai-chang's nose and twisted it hard. Overcome with pain, Pai-chang cried out loudly, "Ow, ow!"
>
> "You say they have flown away," said Ma-Tsu, "but nevertheless they have been here from the very beginning." Sweat broke out from Pai-chang's every pore; he was enlightened on the spot.[117]

Ma-tsu's behavior in this situation must seem strange, queer, and indeed puzzling to people who have little insight into the truth of Zen. Rational thinkers, who primarily use their intellects to judge Zen, would consider it to be utterly illogical and absurd.

The basis for understanding Zen is and will always be our own experience. Mere belief in the truth inherent in us will not get us very far. We must actually live and see it for ourselves. This is why people who seek out a master with the hope that the truth will be revealed to them are bitterly disappointed when the master is unable to show it. A master can only point out the way and set our sight in the right direction, so that we can see and realize it for ourselves. Personal experience is everything in Zen; it is an absolute necessity in dealing with life as a pure experience of being. Without this experience, we will never be able to understand anything that relates to the deeper meaning of our being.

There once was a Zen monk who desperately implored his master to help him in his search for the secret of Zen. The latter gave him this reply:

"I will be glad to help you in any way I can; but there are some things I cannot help you with. These you must see to yourself." The young monk expressed his wish to learn what sort of things these were. "For example, when you are hungry and thirsty," said the master, "your stomach will not be filled if I eat and drink; you must eat and drink yourself. If nature calls, you must tend to this yourself, as I cannot assist you there. And moreover, you are the only one who can carry your body along the path of life."[118]

This friendly piece of advice suddenly opened the mind of the monk for the truth of Zen, and he was so swept away by this realization that he did not know how to express his joy and gratitude.

Most people usually expect to gain an understanding of Zen from a master or books. This expectation is the root of all our uncertainty about Zen. Since we do not have enough trust in our inherent Buddha-nature, we find ourselves in a state of constant doubt and conflict with ourselves. We search for the interior in the exterior and thus further distance ourselves from our true self. The Tibetan sage Padmasambhava (8th century) gives us the following example:

It is quite impossible to find the Buddha anywhere other than in one's own mind. A person who is ignorant of this may seek externally, but how is it possible to find oneself through seeking anywhere other than in oneself?

Someone who seeks their own nature externally is like a fool who, giving a performance in the middle of a crowd, forgets who he is and then seeks everywhere else to find himself.[119]

"Why do you go out?" Meister Eckhart asks us. "Why do you

not stay within yourselves and draw on your own treasure? For you have the whole truth in its essence within you."

THE ENLIGHTENMENT OF LIN-CHI

L et us now take a closer look at a very characteristic example of the spiritual teaching methods of the early Chinese Zen masters.

One of the most important and powerful Zen masters of the 9th century was Lin-chi. His teaching method was one of utmost directness. He uncompromisingly shattered all religious conventions and swept everything aside that barred direct access to the truth. Practical techniques, in the form of blows with the fist and stick, characterized the way along which Lin-chi led his students to the immediate experience of their true being, to enlightenment. He beat them and yelled at them because he learned through experience with his master, Huang-po, that this form of instruction leads more swiftly and more certainly to its aim than do long-winded and wordy explanations.

The story of Lin-chi's enlightenment is told in *Lin-chi-lu* (Record of the Words of Lin-chi), which, together with later collections of koans, is one of the most important Zen texts.

As a young monk, Lin-chi spent three years in Huang-po's monastery without ever having spoken to the master. His mind was so filled with the longing for enlightenment that his concentration caught the attention of the head monk, Mu-chou. The latter urged him to seek out the master and ask him a question. Since Lin-chi could not think of a question, the head monk advised him to ask about the essential meaning of Buddhism.

Thus heartened, Lin-chi finally mustered enough courage to enter Huang-po's room for the first time and put forth his question to the master. Without a word, the master seized his stick and gave Lin-chi a thrashing. Deeply distressed, Lin-chi returned to the head monk and told him what had occurred. Upon the head monk's advice, he went to Huang-po a second and third time, only to receive the same answer. Lin-chi did not understand its meaning and came to believe that he must have bad karma. He finally decided to leave the monastery and search for another master. He told the head monk of his intentions and went with him to bid farewell to Huang-po. "You do not need to travel far," said

Huang-po. "Go to master Ta-yu by the river Kao-an; he will explain it to you!"

So Lin-chi proceeded to Ta-yu's monastery and told the master what had happened. Ta-yu said, "Huang-po treated you with the kindness of an old grandmother. Why have you come here to ask me whether you are at fault?" With these words, Lin-chi suddenly experienced enlightenment and saw everything anew. Joyfully he cried, "From the very beginning there was not much to Huang-po's Buddhism." Ta-yu grabbed him and said, "You little bed-wetter! Just a moment ago you asked me whether you were at fault and now you say there is not much to Huang-po's Buddhism. What have you seen? Quickly, speak! Speak!" Lin-chi immediately punched Ta-yu three times hard in the ribs. At last Ta-yu acknowledged the monk's enlightenment, which he attributed to Huang-po by saying, "Your teacher is Huang-po. This is all his business; it has nothing to do with me."

Lin-chi left Ta-yu and returned to his master. When Huang-po saw him coming he remarked, "When will there be an end to this rascal's coming and going?" "I have returned on account of your grandmotherly kindness," was Lin-chi's answer. Huang-po immediately recognized what had happened to his student, but he concealed his joy over the anticipated favorable outcome. "Where have you come from?" he asked. Lin-chi then told him what had transpired. "Just wait until Ta-yu gets here," said Huang-po, "I'll let that old chatterbox have it." "What are you waiting for? What's the difference?" said Lin-chi, landing Huang-po a blow.

Huang-po was secretly much amused. All the same, he preserved his bearing as a master and screamed, "A lunatic has come to pull at the beard hairs of the tiger!" Lin-chi bellowed, "HO!" Huang-po called in the head monk and said, "Take this madman to the monks' quarters; he is to stay here."

The thrashings Huang-po gave his student may seem unwarranted to the reader who is unacquainted with the teaching methods of Zen. All the same, there is good reason for the saying in Zen: "The eye of enlightenment opens under a hail of thirty blows." And if we consider that the way to liberation is a matter of life and death, we must also admit that it is not a place for polite affectations. According to an old Zen saying: "The matter life and death is enormous, and mortality quickly grabs hold."

Each moment that we live is a divine gift and a singular opportunity for realization; we can never know if we will be capable of drawing the next breath. Real masters are fully cognizant of this and therefore never reassure their students with polite babble. Instead, they constantly challenge their students, who will feel hurt and misunderstood until they finally see through the sneaky tricks of their egos. In the long run, only those who are earnestly committed to seeking the truth and are willing to risk everything for it, including their own life, will be able to endure the difficult process of purification. A story from India makes this point:

With a cloth-covered basket on top of his head, a street vendor made his way through the marketplace calling out loudly, "Truth for sale, truth for sale!" A man approached him and asked, "How much for your truth?" "Your head," came the astonishing reply. "What do you mean? I certainly can't give you my head!" exclaimed the other, appalled. The vendor responded, "You will never obtain the truth unless you are willing to sacrifice everything for it."

Competent masters endeavor to push their students to the limits of their abilities. Regardless of how they treat their students, their actions serve only to further the spiritual maturation process. The masters' great love for their students, with whom they suffer and endure all, is hidden beneath all the apparent toughness.

In everything masters say and do, they are always themselves. They give of themselves just as they are, not conforming to any mold and free of all predictable actions. Students entangled in the vines of endless patterns of thought and behavior are certain to be bewildered and mystified by the master's unbound being.

FALSE GURUS

The enigmatic nature of the master is very tempting for false gurus, or self-proclaimed "masters," to use to their advantage. At present, the urgent need for true masters makes it easy for false gurus to come into play and accounts for the huge number of self-proclaimed masters today. My master, Soji Enku, commented more than once with a hidden smile, "It's a wonder that I have any students at all, since these days everyone wants to be master."

It is a sign of our times that the commercially driven invasion of the pseudo-gurus from the East and West alike, with its many means of promotion, has put the honest work of serious masters in danger of being misunderstood and rejected. Those who nowadays decide to become students of a spiritual master cannot be warned strongly enough against impulsively and all too hastily entrusting themselves to the care of any spiritual guide. We should carefully weigh the risk of placing our fate entirely into the hands of any specific person and should recall the forewarning of Jesus:

> Take heed that you are not led astray! For many will come in my name, saying, "I am he!" and, "The time is at hand!" Do not go after them! [Luke 21:8].

> For false messiahs and false prophets will arise and show signs and wonders [Mark 13:22].

Grave dangers lurk in the trend toward the unreserved veneration of gurus. These become even graver when guru cultism expands at a time of euphoric new age glitter. Religious sects emerge everywhere and esoteric groups pop up like mushrooms out of the ground. In this environment of spiritual confusion (but also of honest spiritual search), clever managers and psychologists clothed as gurus jump at the chance to capture a piece of the spiritual market. Hoards of gurus pour forth from the East, making it even more difficult for the spiritually unprepared to discern the real masters from the charlatans.

The vast majority of gurus consist of the blind leading the blind. Supported by swarms of disciples whose job it is to publicize the eminence and holiness of their lord and master, they easily con their gullible public.

We should note, however, that true masters are as rare in the East as they are in the West. Soji Enku once equated the search for a true master with "a search for a needle in a haystack." Even in Japan, the land of Zen, genuine Zen masters are scarce these days.

The lack of true masters has always been a problem. Chinese Zen master Joshu complained in the 9th century:

> But how is it now? The so-called masters are like so many secondary branches and vines growing further away from the main stems. As they descend further and further away from the great sages, each generation becomes worse than the preceding.

Nowadays I observe yellow-mouthed, inexperienced ones showing themselves openly in public and discoursing on varieties of subjects. They receive offerings and are reverently treated by their followers, even numbering as many as three or five hundred; they claim to be worthy masters and call others their pupils.[120]

These words could have been spoken today. There have always been individuals who claim to lead others to enlightenment while sitting in the dark themselves. Those who have not experienced the reality of their true being and whose minds are still obscured will never be able to free others from the darkness. Whoever presumes to speak of enlightenment without having experienced it is like a blind person attempting to describe the ceiling of the Sistine Chapel. In the *Katha Upanishad* we read:

The truth of the self cannot be fully understood when taught by an ignorant man, for opinions regarding it, not founded in knowledge, vary one from another. Subtler than the subtlest is this self, and beyond all logic. Taught by a teacher who knows the self and Brahman as one, a man leaves vain theory behind and attains to truth.[121]

However, there is nothing wrong with yet "unawakened" individuals striving honestly to convey basic knowledge of spiritual life—inasmuch as they understand it themselves—to beginners on the spiritual path. There are many experienced followers of the spiritual way who possess the ability to make a deep impression on others and inspire them to change their lives and renounce their heretofore materialistic, world-oriented life-style. But although such teachers can be of great spiritual help to students, they will be unable to lead them to higher spiritual levels. At best they will only be able to bring their students as far as they have come themselves. In any case, it is assumed that such teachers will never pretend to have attained realization or pose as masters, for, "What Jupiter is allowed, will long be forbidden to the ox."

The following story is frequently told by Zen Buddhists to poke fun at fraudulent pseudo-masters, who do not possess true Zen understanding, and to tease naive students for following such Zen impostors.

There once was a monk who called himself the "master of silence." In reality he was a fraud who did not possess true Zen understanding. He had two eloquent monks attend him and help him sell his pseudo-Zen. They answered all questions for him, as he never uttered a word himself in demonstration of his mysterious Zen silence.

One day while his attendants were out, a wandering monk came to him and asked, "Master, what is Buddha?" Not knowing what to do or say, he desperately looked around in all directions—east and west, here and there—in an attempt to see whether the two monks who usually spoke for him had returned.

The wandering monk appeared to be satisfied and further asked, "What is *dharma* [sacred teaching]?" At a loss for an answer, the master of silence looked up at the ceiling and then down at the floor to enlist the help of heaven and hell.

Thereupon the monk posed a third question: "What is *sangha* [sacred community]?" At this, the master of silence could only close his eyes.

Finally the monk asked, "What is a blessing?" Defeated, the false master spread out his hands in a gesture of capitulation. The monk was deeply satisfied with this exchange. He left the master and set off on his way. He soon came across the two attendants and enthusiastically told them how enlightened the master of silence was: "I asked him what Buddha was. He immediately turned his face east and then west to indicate that people must always watch out for Buddha. He then looked here and there to say that Buddha cannot truly be found either in the East or in the West.

Next I asked him what *dharma* was. He looked up and down in reply, which meant that the truth of the *dharma* is a whole, has no equal, and makes no distinction between high and low.

In answer to my question about what *sangha* was,

104

he simply closed his eyes and said nothing. That was a reference to the famous saying, `When one is able to close his eyes and sleep soundly in the deep of the cloud-covered mountains, he is a great monk.'

In response to my last question about what a blessing was, he stretched out his arms and showed me both hands. That meant that the blessings of his helping hands would guide all living beings. What an enlightened master! How profound his teaching!"[122]

ESOTERIC DRUG CULT

The greatest danger for spiritual seekers is represented by yet another sort of false guru who, armed with pseudo-scientific evidence, propagates the use of drugs for achieving a higher level of consciousness. Well-versed in the vocabulary of Eastern mysticism, the blind leading the blind sing their song in praise of psychedelic drugs and zealously spread the word that there is a shortcut on the spiritual way. The primary drug employed by the gurus of this scene (who are mostly psychologists) is lysergic acid diethylamide, LSD for short. Other psychedelic drugs are also used, such as hashish, marijuana, heroin, and mescaline. A main feature of the esoteric drug cult is that the people who praise these psychedelic drugs as a back door to enlightenment lack meditative experience based on serious spiritual schooling.

But why all the euphoric enthusiasm about a chemically induced stupor of pleasant hallucinations and raptures? An essential factor is that these chemicals release the consciousness from the ties that normally bind it. The egocentrically imprisoned and isolated consciousness suddenly feels freed of its bonds, resulting in a state of ecstasy and expanded awareness. This experience of the broadening of a nonjudgmental, chaotic awareness is termed "consciousness expansion" by drug gurus and is equated with the attainment of a higher dimension. It is crucial to understand that this sort of consciousness expansion has absolutely nothing to do with a mystical experience in the sense of spiritual realization. Consciousness expansion is nothing more than a broadening of awareness, just as a pair of glasses improves vision or a hearing aid extends hearing ability. An expansion of consciousness induced by psychedelic drugs is never more than an earthly phenomenon of refined sensual awareness and has nothing in common with the "consciousness intensification" realized during meditation. In his well-known work *Ursprung und Gegenwart* (Origin and Presence), Jean Gebser writes:

> Quantitative increase must never affect the consciousness, whose nature is always qualitative. For this reason alone we stress that we must never make the mistake of aiming for consciousness expansion, when it is really a matter of consciousness intensification. Sheer expansion of consciousness leads to ruin just as does material atomization.[123]

Mere consciousness expansion can, therefore, never be the goal of our spiritual way, for which there are no shortcuts, either in the form of "samadhi pipe smoking" or "satori capsules." The altered states of consciousness induced by psychedelic drugs are ultimately just disturbances of normal consciousness. Beautiful lights may flash, bringing with them an increase in awareness of color and form, and joyful ecstasy may be experienced; yet all this can never be more than the varying effects of a disturbance in consciousness. These feverish, overwrought episodes afford no access to a higher level of consciousness, nor do they have anything to do with a transcendent experience; they can at best be described as pseudo-transcendent adventures.

At first glance, drug episodes and mystical experiences appear to have some things in common. However, this is a colossal misperception. Worlds of difference lie between the experiences of a drug consumer and those of a mystic. Furthermore, drug-induced alterations in consciousness cause a dulling of the intellect, resulting in a partial, if not total, loss of critical faculties. This loss can even lead to a complete breakdown of personality.

Psychedelic drug users sacrifice their capacity for spiritual development through the destruction of the psychical-physical energy source upon which their inner growth depends. Having delivered themselves into a descending spiral, they sink ever deeper. And the deeper they sink, the harder it will be for them to resurface. Eventually, the strength they need to resurface will be completely lost. On this point, Buddhist scholar Lama Anagarika Govinda says:

> LSD (and other psychedelic drugs) leads away from the center in an ever further splintering multitude of unrelated and constantly changing projections of unconscious content. Momentarily capturing our attention, they turn us into completely passive observers of the unreeling of a psychical film strip in which we take no part. The longer we give ourselves up to them, the more certain they will suffocate all creative impulses needed by our own effort for its realization.[124]

Many who have sought to force open the secret gate to the truth with chemical means have had to pay for it with mental illness or brain damage. Psychiatric institutions are full of "drug mystics" who were thoroughly convinced they had found a route to enlightenment. Without the necessary spiritual maturity, those who seek to enter the realm of profound universal consciousness will be devoured by it and lose themselves in the chaos of their self-made madness.

THE NECESSITY OF THE MASTER

I have often been asked whether it is absolutely necessary to have a master. My answer is that very few have come to realize their true being without one. Of these few, the most famous is the Indian sage Ramana Maharshi, who died in 1950. At the age of seventeen he awoke to his true self without the aid of a master.

One day he was sitting alone in his room when he was suddenly and unequivocally stricken with the terror of death. He felt that his time had come. The feeling overtook him with an inconceivable force and filled him with great fear. There was nothing in his past that could possibly have explained the fear of death he felt at that moment. His entire consciousness was filled with the single thought: "I am moving towards death. I must die now." He lay down on the floor and watched as life slipped out of his body. Sight, hearing, smell, and touch vanished. His thoughts darkened and his ego-consciousness dissolved. At precisely the moment his consciousness disappeared, the consciousness of his truc self shone forth with incredible power and liberating clarity. But such experiences are extremely rare. And considering that only a few come to enlightenment, even among those who practice under the guidance of a competent master, we should not be too quick to dispense with the help of a master. Zen master Huang-po said:

> Ah, be diligent! Be diligent! Of a thousand or ten thousand attempting to enter by this gate, only three or perhaps five pass through.[125]

It is entirely possible that the reader of these lines is a divinely blessed exception, as was the Indian sage Ramana Maharshi. All the same, we should hesitate to be overconfident. We are better off assuming that if we rely solely on books, we are in constant danger of becoming further entangled in the snarl of our own speculations and suppositions, as are those who align themselves with unqualified teachers.

A student who has the good fortune of being taken on by a real master must meet two basic prerequisites: absolute trust and surrender. Without these, it will be impossible for the master to guide the student properly. Surrender to the master should never lead to the intellectual paralysis or total slavery of the student. Otherwise, Christ would not have said, "The truth shall make you free" (John 8:32).

Students must also preserve beginner's spirit, which means that regardless of how much they know, they accept that they really know nothing. It all boils down to one thing: Those who seek a master must spiritually empty themselves; if they do not, they could fare like the student in the following example:

> Once a young philosopher who was proud of his scholastic knowledge went to visit a Zen master at his monastery to ask to become his student. When he was led into the master's room and had taken his seat, the young man was, as was customary, served tea by an attendant. The master instructed the monk, "Why don't you pour more tea into the cup?" The attendant monk did as instructed, and when he was about to stop pouring, the master insisted, "More, more!" The cup was now full to the brim and the monk could

pour no more tea into it. The master, however, still sternly demanded, "More, more!"

The young guest could not remain silent, and spoke out, "It overflows, master!" The master then quietly said to him, "When one wants to learn anything from others, he first has to empty himself; otherwise there is no room for the teaching to enter. You had better go home now." The young man was ashamed of himself at these words, and with this began sincerely to seek for the truth.[126]

THE INEVITABILITY OF DEATH

The first step on the way to becoming Zen students involves emptying ourselves. This does not imply, as so many mistakenly assume, rendering ourselves submissive and keeping our deceptive consciousness still and unmoved, so that it remains free of identification and clinging, but rather something much deeper and more meaningful. It calls for us to look our own helplessness, in relation to being chained to and caught in the cycle of birth and death, straight in the eye. We should each have a clear picture of our situation and be constantly aware of the meaninglessness of our worldly endeavors in view of our own mortality.

"Nothing is important in the face of death!" I often heard Soji Enku speak these words. The inevitability of death is an undeniable fact. One day we will die.

It is therefore of vital importance that spiritual seekers cultivate an alertness at all times to the unpredictability of the time of death. Of course, we all know that we must die someday, but most of us have put the thought that death could come now, within the next hour, far out of our minds. We must nevertheless accept the fact that life's power can slip away from us as quickly as a dewdrop from the tip of a blade of grass. Human life is as fragile as a soap bubble. We would thus be foolish to make the fatal mistake of delaying practicing the spiritual way, with the excuse of being momentarily too busy and wanting to wait until we have more time.

Death will surprise us unexpectedly, whether or not we are prepared for it. At this crucial moment, we will realize that all learning, power, and wealth, in other words, everything to which we had devoted our lives, is powerless to help us. When death touches us, we can do no more. It yanks everything out of our hands. It destroys our abilities to plan and control and is so radically thorough that everything that was before becomes nothing, as if it never existed: joy and sorrow, gain and loss, love and hate. Everything that filled our lives is swept away. Death shreds to pieces all of our self-deceptions about the importance of everyday things in our human existence. The only thing of value at the hour of death is what we have attained along the spiritual way.

In Thomas Kempis's 15th-century work, *The Imitation of Christ*, we find a highly significant passage, reminiscent of the teaching of Tibetan Buddhism:

> Mortals, think of dying! Very quickly there will be an end of you here, so be aware of your situation. Today man is here, tomorrow he has disappeared. And when he is out of sight, he is also quickly out of mind.
>
> You ought so to order yourself in all your thoughts and deeds, as if today you were about to die. If today you are not prepared, how will you be so tomorrow? Tomorrow is uncertain, and how do you know that you shall live until tomorrow?
>
> Therefore be always in a state of readiness, and lead your life that death may never take you unprepared, "for the son of man is coming at an hour you do not expect" [Luke 12:40].
>
> Labor now so to live, that at the hour of death you may rejoice rather than fear.
>
> Learn now to die to the world, and to despise all earthly things, that you may freely go to Christ.
>
> Ah! foolish one, why do you think to live long, when you are not certain of a single day?
>
> How many have been deceived with false hope and unexpectedly snatched away from the world!
>
> Thus death comes to all, and man's life swiftly passes away like a shadow.[127]

This calls to mind the admonishing words of Buddha to his disciples:

This world will come to pass and all that is important will fly away. We must each awaken from our dream. There is no time to lose. Therefore, be steadfast in resolve!

Everything in the world is impermanent like autumn clouds. The birth and death of living beings are like the scenes in a theatrical play. Human life is like a flash of lightning and like the waters of a mountain stream.[128]

Release of self springs out of the bitter experience of the impermanence of all being. It rises up out of the depths of our own helplessness and consequent surrender. When we let go of ourselves and thereby lay ourselves completely in the hands of the divine, the divine light of our true being will all at once shine forth. In the words of Zen master Bassui (14th century):

All at once your mind will burst forth into great enlightenment and you will feel as though you have risen from the dead, laughing loudly and clapping your hands in delight. Now for the first time you will know that mind itself is Buddha.[129]

Experiencing our original nature beyond birth and death represents the great awakening from the dream of a three-dimensional world limited by space and time. All things suddenly fall away and we are free to see the world as it really is, as if for the first time. All duality of subject and object vanishes in this wonderful clarity of consciousness, and we feel as if we have been relieved of a crushing burden.

In the letter of Chinese Zen master Yuan-wu quoted earlier, there is a very good description of this indescribable state of consciousness:

Your very existence has been delivered from all limitations; you have become open, light, and transparent. You gain an illuminating insight into the very nature of things, which now appear to you as so many fairylike flowers having no graspable realities. Here is manifested the unsophisticated self which is the original face of your being; here is shown all bare the most beautiful landscape of your birthplace. There is but

111

one straight passage open and unobstructed through and through. This is so when you surrender all—your body, your life, and all that belongs to your inmost self. This is where you gain peace, ease, nondoing, and inexpressible delight. All the sutras and sastras are no more than communications of this fact; all sages, ancient as well as modern, have exhausted their ingenuity and imagination to no other purpose than to point the way to this.

It is like unlocking a door to a treasury; when the entrance is once gained, every object coming into your view is yours, every opportunity that presents itself is available for your use; for are they not, however multitudinous, all possessions obtainable within the original being of yourself? Every treasure there is but waiting your pleasure and utilization. This is what is meant by "Once gained, eternally gained, even unto the end of time." Yet there really is nothing gained; what you have gained is no gain, and yet all is truly gained in this.[130]

CHAPTER NINE

The Zen Way:
Free Yourselves of Everything

GRASPING THE TRUTH DIRECTLY

The preceding chapters should make clear that freeing ourselves from the cycle of birth and death should never be equated with disdaining the world, but instead with releasing ourselves from our clinging to it. We must first let everything go in order to get everything back at a new level.

True masters constantly challenge their students to rid themselves of the clouds of ignorance, of all bonds and illusions, so that they can awaken to their true self, naked of all else. Any device may be used to drive students to the brink of no return, where they have no choice but to let go or to summon all their might to hold on to their dreamworld.

It should be of no surprise that students in this situation are more likely to hold on to various patterns of behavior and thought than to release their hold. There are even students who cling to the belief of having let go:

One day a monk said to Zen master Joshu: "I have

cast away everything, and there is nothing at all left in my mind. What would you say to that?" To this Joshu gave the unexpected reply: "Cast it away!" The monk insisted, "I have told you that there is nothing left in me. What should I cast away?" Joshu then said, "In that case, keep on carrying it."[131]

We will be unable to awaken to the reality of the one mind until we have freed ourselves of all thoughts and ideas about letting go. Our letting go must become our forgetting. Everything must be forgotten: Buddha, enlightenment, *dharma*, Zen, whatever. These concepts are just empty words with no real value. We will be incapable of attaining a direct experience of our true being as long as we depend on them.

A monk asked his master, "Please show me the way without appealing to words of mouth." To this the master gave his answer, "Ask me without using words of mouth."[132]

Zen demands that we negate everything, regardless of what it is—even including negation itself. The slightest trace of negation or affirmation means we are still thousands of miles away from the truth of Zen. Those who affirm or deny are lost. Such people stand outside of Zen, or as Zen master Bassui put it: "Whatever you say is wrong. And if you say nothing, you are equally wrong." Master I-tuan explained in one of his sermons:

"To talk is blaspheming, to remain silent is deception. Beyond silence and talking there is an upward passage, but my mouth is not yet wide enough to point it out to you." So saying, he came down from the pulpit.[133]

Yang-shan, one of the great Chinese masters of the 9th century, gave the following sermon:

You monks, turning back your light look within; do not try to memorize my words. Since the beginningless past you have turned your backs to your light, throwing yourselves into the darkness. The root of false thinking goes deeply into the ground; it is hard to pull it out. The many contrivances are meant for the destruction of coarser imaginations. They are like the yellow leaves given to a child to stop its crying. They are in themselves of no value whatever.

[Yet] when I demonstrate Zen in its genuine form, nobody is able to accompany me however much he may desire it; much less a company of five or seven hundred. But when I talk this way and that, they crowd into my room and vie with one another to pick up whatever leavings there are. It is like cheating a child with an empty palm; in truth there is nothing real. The sciences and miracles are not needed at all. Why not? Because such are the fringes of reality. When you want to know mind, penetrate into the very source of things. When all your imaginations, holy and worldly, are exhausted, reality presents itself, true and eternal, in the unity of one and many, and this is where Buddha of Suchness abides.[134]

Master Nan-chan had this exchange with his students:

"As to fine words and exquisite phrases, you have enough of them in other places. If today there is any one in this assembly who has gone even beyond the first principle, let him come forward and say one word. If there is, he has not betrayed our expectations."

A monk asked, "What is the first principle?"
"Why do you not ask the first principle?"
"I am asking it this very moment."
"You have already fallen on a second principle."[135]

Hsuan-sha sat quietly in his pulpit for some time without saying a word. The monks thought he was not going to give them a sermon and began to retire all at once. He then scolded them: "As I observe, you are all of one pattern; not one of you has sagacity enough to see things properly. You have come to see me open my mouth, and, taking hold of my words, imagine they are the ultimate truths. It is a pity that you all fail to know what's what. As long as you remain like this, what a calamity!"[136]

115

Another time the master again remained silent for a while and then said, "I have been thoroughly kind to you, but do you understand?"

A monk asked, "What is the sense of remaining quiet without uttering a word?"

The master said, "How you talk in your sleep."

"I wish you to tell me about the truth of Zen."

"What is the use of snoring?"

"I may snore, but how about you?"

The master said, "How is it possible to be so insensitive as to not know where it itches?"[137]

Keeping silent before an assembly was a favorite device of many masters. Chih-feng, for example, remained completely silent for a while and then called out, "O monks, look, look!" upon which he left his seat.

Master Jui-yen while in the pulpit kept his monks standing for some time, and finally said: "I am ashamed of not having anything special today. But if you are merely here to follow my talk and listen to my voice, you had better indeed retire into the hall and warm yourselves by the fire. Good night, monks."[138]

Chang-ching came up to the pulpit, and seeing all the monks assembled threw his fan down on the floor and said: "Fools take gold for earth, but how about the wise? Future generations are not to be despised. It is not praiseworthy all the time to be too modest. Is there anybody wishing to come out before me?" A monk came out, and making bows withdrew his steps and stood still.

The master said, "Anything besides that?"

"I await your fair judgment."

"A peach-stone one thousand years old!" said the master.[139]

Yang-lung came up to the pulpit, the monks crowded into the hall; the master rose from his seat and danced and said, "Do you understand?"

"No, master," the monks answered.

The master demanded, "I performed, without

116

abandoning my religion, a deed belonging to the world; why do you not understand?"[140]

In the preceding examples we can see that the instructional methods used by the ancient Zen masters consisted of awakening something in the mind of the student that would allow the latter to intuitively grasp the truth of Zen. The following examples will give us a chance to become familiar with a few other unconventional and unusual methods of instruction used by masters. Since it is impossible to understand these methods through intellectualization, they will seem unfathomable to those who have yet to acquire a direct intuitive understanding of Zen.

A monk once asked Master Joshu, "What is the one ultimate word of truth?" Instead of giving him any specific answer he made a simple response saying, "Yes." The monk, who naturally failed to see any sense in this kind of response, asked for a second time, and to this the master roared back, "I am not deaf!"[141]

Another time when Joshu was asked about the "first word," he coughed. The monk remarked, "Is this not it?" "Why, an old man is not even allowed to cough!"—this came quickly from the old master.

Joshu had still another occasion to express his view on the one word. A monk asked, "What is the one word?" Demanded the master, "What do you say?" "What is the one word?" —the question was repeated when Joshu gave his verdict, "You make it two."[142]

Joshu was asked another time, "One light divides itself into hundreds of thousands of lights; may I ask where this one light originates?" The questioner had hardly finished speaking when Joshu simply threw off one of his shoes without a remark.[143]

Ling-yun was once asked, "How were things before the appearance of the Buddha in the world?" The master raised his *hossu* [fly swatter]. "How were things after the appearance of the Buddha?" He again raised the *hossu*.[144]

Raising the *hossu* and the *shippei* (staff) to demonstrate the truth of Zen was a favorite method of the old Zen masters. The *hossu* and the *shippei* were the masters" trademarks, so naturally they used them in responding to students' questions.

> One day Huang-po ascended the pulpit, and as soon as the monks were gathered, the master took up his staff and drove them all out. When they were about all out, he called them, and they turned their heads back. The master said, "The moon looks like a bow, less rain and more wind."[145]

One day Huang-po entered the assembly hall and delivered this sermon to his students:

> "Having many sorts of knowledge cannot compare with giving up seeking for anything, which is the best of all things. Mind is not of several kinds and there is no doctrine which can be put into words. As there is no more to be said, the assembly is dismissed!"[146]

THE ORIGINAL CONDITION OF THE MIND

Traditionally, the essential features of Zen are embodied in four principles:

1. Transmission outside the scriptures

2. No dependence upon words or letters

3. Direct pointing to your own mind

4. Attaining Buddhahood through direct realization of your own nature

Zen exudes self-confidence and tolerates reliance on nothing whatsoever, not even on Buddha, which explains the old Zen saying, "If you should meet the Buddha, slay him!" In other words, let nothing, no matter how sacred and full of philosophical wisdom it is, come between you and the immediate experience of your true being.

Zen is the highest and most direct teaching, one in which there is absolutely nothing to do or learn. It is the way that leads to immediate and instantaneous grasping of reality, just as it is. The only prerequisite is that we be able to let everything go at once and die the great death.

Zen has nothing to do with hairsplitting philosophical deliberation or logical reasoning. That is why Chinese Zen master Ta-hui warns us:

> Conceptualization is a deadly obstacle for a Zen yogi, more dangerous than poisonous snakes or wild animals. People of powerful intellect are virtually always possessed with the desire to convert everything into mental concepts; they are never able to completely free themselves of this in any of their activities. As months and years go by this craving grows even stronger. Without their realizing it, the mind and conceptualization gradually become inseparable. Those who desire to free themselves of it discover that it is impossible.
>
> That is why I say poisonous snakes and wild animals can be avoided, but there is no way of evading intellectual conceptualization.[147]

The fundamental idea of Zen tells us to take the direct and shortest way to the experience of our true being without recourse to anything external or supplementary. That is why Zen rejects everything that has the least to do with external authority; it tends only to absolute trust in the inner nature of human beings. All authority in Zen comes from within and is independent of stipulated religious dogmas of any kind. A Christian can live in Zen as well as a Buddhist, for Zen is not a religion among others, but rather the true foundation of all religions. Zen opens our eyes to the great mystery of our universal nature. It gives us access to the unending inner space, which manifests itself to us in spatial infinity and timeless eternity.

Inexpressible in words, the truth of Zen has nothing to do with pious behavior and sanctimonious holiness. It is always immediate and direct. With utmost emphasis, it points straight to our own hearts without becoming caught up in conventions and ideas. It is free, and without this freedom it loses its spontaneity and freshness and becomes as lifeless as an empty shell.

Embroilment in assorted religious beliefs and philosophical

speculation prevents most people who search for the secret of being from realizing the truth of their own mind. Searching for an external truth and regarding it as an object identifiable by a subject conform to the dualistic reasoning of intellectual comprehension. Since the truth pervades our very being and all that surrounds us, it is impossible for us to distinguish or separate ourselves from it. Therefore, our only choice is to attain to an immediate awareness of that which is and always will be present in and around us, our most intrinsic true being.

A Buddhist text of the Tibetan master Milarepa (12th century) says:

> When a person's own mind recalls the original condition of the mind, all deceptive thoughts melt away by themselves in the realm of the ultimate reality.
>
> There is no longer anyone who causes suffering and no one who suffers. The most exhaustive study of the sutras teaches us no more than this.... Those who are able to perceive their mind—without becoming distracted—have no more need of words or idle talk. Those who are able to immerse themselves in the awareness of their true self no longer need to sit stiffly like a corpse. Having realized the essence of all manifestations, all their desires will fade away on their own into nothing.[148]

If everyone were conscious of the true nature of their mind, they would realize that the world of their sensual awareness— including the concepts and intellectual reflexes generated by this awareness—constitutes but a tiny portion of their mind. They would recognize that at the moment in which they relinquish all arbitrary notions, they will be open to endless and unforeseen dimensions of consciousness. The boundlessness of universal consciousness would unfold itself to them. Huang-po expresses it with the following words:

> This pure mind, the source of everything, shines forever and on all with the brilliance of its own perfection. But the people of the world do not awake to it, regarding only that which sees, hears, feels, and knows as mind. Blinded by their own sight, hearing, feeling

and knowing, they do not perceive the spiritual brilliance of the source-substance. If they would only eliminate all conceptual thought in a flash, that source-substance would manifest itself like the sun ascending through the void and illuminating the whole universe without bounds. Therefore, if you students of the way seek to progress through seeing, hearing, feeling and knowing, when you are deprived of your perceptions, your way to the mind will be cut off and you will find nowhere to enter.

Only realize that, though real mind is expressed in these perceptions, it neither forms part of them nor is separate from them. You should not start reasoning from these perceptions, nor allow them to give rise to conceptual thought; yet nor should you seek the one mind apart from them or abandon them in your pursuit of the *dharma*. Do not keep them nor abandon them nor dwell in them nor cleave to them. Above, below and around you, all is spontaneously existing, for there is nowhere which is outside the Buddha-mind.[149]

THE KOAN "MU"

The historical meaning of the Japanese word *koan* is roughly "the place where the truth is declared." In Zen, a koan is a paradox or problem that is insoluble by means of discursive thought. Most koans are the sayings of the great Zen masters of the past, who used them on their students to open their minds to the truth of Zen. Here are a few examples:

A cow is going through a grated window. Horns, head and four legs have passed through. Why can't its tail pass?

A monk asked Joshu, "All things return to the one, but where does this one return to?"

Joshu replied, "When I lived in Ching-chou, I had a robe made that weighed seven pounds."

A monk asked Joshu, "What is the meaning of the

121

Patriarch's coming from the West?"
Joshu said, "The cypress tree in the courtyard."

A monk asked Tung-chan, "Who is the Buddha?"
"Three pounds of flax" was the answer.

The striking characteristic of almost all koans is the illogical, absurd sense of the words or action. The masters' answers to their students' questions are confusing and make us wonder what relation they actually have to the questions. It is important to understand that the Zen masters' remarks have nothing to do with conceptual or analytical observations within the usual confines of a logical dualism. They are instead an expression of a tremendous experience of such an all-embracing universality, that it cannot be contained within the bounds of space and time or represented within the limitations of words.

The Zen practitioner's key to dealing with a koan is to have acquired the same utterly clear state of consciousness as that from which the koan was issued and which is unattainable through logical analysis. The profound truth that lay hidden in the koan will only become evident once the mind of the student is ripe enough to be completely in tune with the mind of the master who gave the koan.

Let us turn now to the koan MU. This koan is doubtless the most famous of all and is the one most often used by Japanese Zen masters of today:

A monk once asked Master Joshu, "Has a dog Buddha-nature or not?"
Joshu said, "MU!"[150]

The Chinese character for *Mu* literally means "nothing." Joshu's answer was quite simply "Nothing," which was not to say that a dog lacks Buddha-nature. Naturally, both Joshu and the monk knew that Buddha-nature is inherent in all creatures without exception, which is why Joshu's "MU" should never be interpreted as a denial of this fact. The only purpose of his response was to break the monk of rational thinking in trying to understand the truth of Zen and to get him to aspire to a higher understanding of reality beyond affirmation and negation, in which all contradictions disappear on their own.

Joshu's "MU" is neither a yes nor a no. It is an answer that surpasses the opposition of yes and no and directly points to Buddha-nature, to the reality beyond yes and no. Joshu's own experience of Buddha-nature finds its creative expression in his "MU" and powerfully points to the incomparable enlightenment attainable only through leaving behind discriminating thought. Not until we are willing to take this step and throw ourselves into the abyss of great doubt (see chapter six) will the fullness of divine nothing reveal itself.

Those who are unwilling to do this and believe they can solve the koan MU through deductive reasoning will only spin their wheels and not gain an inch on MU. Clinging to words and expressions and attempting to interpret and understand MU intellectually is like trying to hit the moon with a stick, or trying to relieve an itch on your foot by scratching your shoe. The old masters said, "Attempting to solve MU by rational means is like attempting to break through an iron wall with your fist."

What, then, is the deeper meaning of Joshu's "MU"? The answer can only be, "Anything I could say would miss the truth," or in Huang-po's words, "All conceptual thinking is erroneous belief, and the nondoubting of words a great disease. Why base a discussion on false terms?" Therefore, all who desire to solve the koan or problem of MU have no other choice but to delve into MU with all their being, until they become completely one with it. Zen master Mumon (13th century) gives us the following advice in his commentary on Joshu's "MU":

> In the practice of Zen you must pass through the barrier set up by the old masters. To realize enlightenment, you must cut off all discriminating thoughts. If you cannot pass through the barrier of the ancient masters, you are like a ghost who haunts the bushes and trees.
>
> What, then, is this barrier set by the ancient masters? It is none other than MU, the one gateway to Zen. That is why it is called the gateless gate of Zen. One who has passed through this gate cannot only clearly see Joshu face to face, but can walk hand in hand will all the masters of the past. Standing eyebrow to eyebrow, he sees with the same eyes and hears with the same ears. How marvelous! Who would not wish to pass through this wonderful gate?

Therefore you must concentrate on MU with every one of your 360 bones and 84,000 pores and transform your bodies into one great search. Apply yourselves day and night to MU and do not attempt nihilistic or dualistic interpretations. You must reach the point where you feel as if you have swallowed a red-hot iron ball. You are unable to spit it out, no matter how hard you try. Completely extinguish all illusory thoughts and discriminations along with the feelings you have pampered till now. If you practice in this manner, MU will ripen, and inside and outside will become as one. You will be like a mute who has had a dream but is unable to talk about it.

Suddenly you break through the barrier of MU. You will astound the heavens and shake the earth. As though having seized the sword of General Kan, you would slay the Buddha should you meet him. If you were to encounter an old master, you would kill him. Facing life and death, you will rejoice in utter freedom. In all realms of existence and modes of birth you will move about in a samadhi of innocent delight.

How then, should you concentrate on MU? Devote all your strength wholeheartedly to MU. If you continue this way without intermission, your mind will suddenly become bright, like a burning candle that illuminates the entire universe.[151]

At the end of this thorough commentary on Joshu's "MU," Mumon attached a short verse to express MU once more. It is very direct and to the point:

Dog! Buddha-nature!
The truth is plain to see.
One instant of "yes" or "no"
Life and limb are lost.[152]

Master Mumon teaches us in a very insistent yet kindhearted way how to proceed with the koan MU in the practice of Zen. The commentary comes from his superb work, *Mumonkan*, a collection of 48 koans. Mumon relentlessly practiced with the koan MU for six years. Finally one day, upon hearing the beat of the great monastery drum to indicate midday, he suddenly realized profound enlightenment. The intensity of this enlightenment experience is conveyed in a verse he wrote shortly thereafter:

> A thunderclap in a clear blue sky!
> All earthly creatures have opened their eyes.
> Everything beneath the sun bowed at once.
> Mount Sumeru jumps up and dances.[153]

A little while later, after his master (Yueh-lin) confirmed his enlightenment, he wrote another short poem with five-syllable lines:

> MU MU MU MU MU
> MU MU MU MU MU
> MU MU MU MU MU
> MU MU MU MU MU[154]

DO NOT BE DECEIVED

One of the most awesome and powerful figures in the history of Zen was Lin-chi, about whose dramatic first encounter with his master Huang-po we heard in the preceding chapter. With Lin-chi and other Tang dynasty masters of his lineage, Chinese Zen Buddhism reached its pinnacle and, at the same time, its end. Lin-chi was an unusual personality of great stature, a master of radical consequence and uncompromising directness. He ruthlessly cleared everything away that barred direct access to the truth. Let us look at an example of one his extraordinary sermons:

> Students today lack self-confidence; they should not seek externally. As long as you continue to rely upon the methods of the ancestors, you will never be able to distinguish between true and false. Buddhas and the ancient masters are nothing more than the tracks left behind by their teachings. Then come people who pluck a saying out of them, regardless of whether its meaning is clear to them or remains hidden. They become uncertain, look up at the sky and down at the earth, ask others for advice and remain confused all the same.

Buddha's law requires no effort. It exists in the everyday and has no aim: shitting, pissing, getting dressed, eating, and sleeping when you are tired. The simple-minded may laugh at me, but the wise know better.

You tell the world over, "Whoever practices will become enlightened." Do not deceive yourselves with this! If anything is to be gained by practice, then it is the fate of birth and death.. . .

Buddha and the ancient masters were people with no special intention. Certain blind baldies, to be sure, practice meditation and the observance of rules. They pack up their thoughts and desires and never let go of them; they shun clamor and seek quiet. That has nothing to do with the truth [of Zen]. Such and the like are mere affectations. Do not be deceived![155]

We will end our book with a helpful hint from this venerable Zen master Lin-chi. He tells us how we can attain what we have always had because it was never lost: perfect enlightenment.

Friends, I say to you: There is no Buddha, no doctrine, no instruction and no realization. What are you chasing after so embittered? Do you want to set another head on top of your own, you blind blockheads? Your head is right where it should be. So what are you lacking? You who follow the way are no different from the Buddhas and patriarchs. But you don't believe it and so you turn in your search to the outside. Do not be deceived! Outside there is nothing to be gained. Instead of hanging on to my words, you should set yourselves at ease and search no further. Do not hang on to the past and do not long for the future. That is better than a ten–year pilgrimage.[156]

126

Notes

Translator's remarks: The biblical quotations in the original German edition of this book come from the following versions: Einheitsübersetzung, Luther-Bibel (old and new editions), Elberfelder Bibel, and Jerusalemer Bibel. They have been rendered into English with diligent comparison to the King James, New King James, Revised Standard, and Phillips Modern English versions, the New English Bible, and the Jerusalem Bible.

An asterisk indicates titles used in preparation of the English translation that are different from those given by the author in the original German version of this book. All quotations from works with German titles have been rendered into English by the translator.

CHAPTER 1. THE UNIVERSALITY OF THE MIND

1. Garma C. C. Chang, *The Buddhist Teaching of Totality* (University Park, Pa.: Pennsylvania State University Press, 1971), pp. 175-76.

2. Ibid., p. 173.

3. Ibid., pp. 179-80.

4. Prabhavananda and Frederick Manchester, ed. and trans., *The Upanishads: Breath of the Eternal* (New York: New American Library/Penguin USA, 1975), p. 81.

5. Fritjof Capra, *The Tao of Physics* (London: Flamingo, 1975), p. 220 (Bhagavad-Gita 9, 7-9).

6. SchPej Ohasama and August Faust, *Zen* (Darmstadt: Wissenschaftliche Buchgesellschaft, 1968), p. 62.

7. John Blofeld, trans., *The Zen Teaching of Huang Po on the Transmission of the Mind* (New York: Grove Weidenfeld, Grove Press, 1959), pp. 35-36.

Chapter 2. THE DEPERSONIFICATION OF THE PERSONALITY

8. Nyanatiloka, *Buddhistisches Wörterbuch* (Constance: Verlag Christiani, 1952), p. 109.

127

9. Blofeld, *Huang Po*, pp. 45-46.
10. Lama Anagarika Govinda, *Creative Meditation and Multi-Dimensional Consciousness* (London: George Allen & Unwin, 1977), p. 199.
11. Henri Le Saux, *Die Gegenwart Gottes erfahren* (Mainz: Matthias-Grünewald-Verlag, 1980), p. 103 (*Katha Upanishad* 6, 12).
12. Blofeld, *Huang Po*, p. 35.
13. Heinrich Dumoulin, *Begegnung mit dem Buddhismus* (Freiburg: Herder Verlag, 1978), p. 59.
14. Henri Le Saux, *Der Weg zum anderen Ufer* (Cologne: Diederichs Verlag, 1980), p. 62 (Katha Upanishad 2, 18).
15. *M. O'C. Walshe, trans. and ed., *Meister Eckhart: Sermons & Treatises* (Longmead: Element Books, 1987), III, p. 275.
16. Le Saux, *Ufer*, p. 63 (*Mandukya Upanishad* 6).
17. Le Saux, Ibid., p. 64 (*Chandogya Upanishad* 7, 23-25).
18. Hugo M. Enomiya-Lassalle, *Zen und christliche Mystik* (Freiburg : Aurum Verlag, 1986), p. 275.
19. Hans Torwesten, Vedanta (Freiburg : Walter-Verlag, 1985), p. 68.

Chapter 3. THE WAY TO LIBERATION

20. Bettina Bäumer, *Befreiung zum Sein* (Einsiedeln: Benzinger Verlag, 1986), p. 218 (Katha Upanishad II 4, 2).
21. Kallistos Ware, *The Orthodox Way* (Crestwood, N.Y.: St. Vladimir's Press, 1981), p. 87.
22. Otto Betz, *Der Humor Jesu und die Fröhlichkeit der Christen* (Ulm: Süddeutsche Verlagsgesellschaft, 1981), p. 28.
23. Blanche Christine Olschak, *Die Heiterkeit der Seele* (Frauenfeld: Verlag im Waldgut, 1988), p. 17.
24. Alla Selawry, *Das immerwährende Herzensgebet* (Munich: O. W. Barth Verlag, 1980), p. 94.
25. Kallistos Ware and Emmanuel Jungclaussen, *Hinführung zum Herzensgebet* (Freiburg: Herder Verlag, 1982), p. 69.
26. *Based on Walshe, *Meister Eckhart*, II, 196, and Josef Quint, ed. & trans., *Meister Eckhart: Deutsche Predigten und Traktate* (Munich: Hanser Verlag, 1963), p. 312.
27. Dietmar Mieth, *Meister Eckhart* (Freiburg: Walter-Verlag, 1979), p. 277.
28. *Walshe, *Meister Eckhart*, vol. 3, pp. 14-15.
29. Hans Wolfgang Schumann, *Buddhismus* (Freiburg: Walter-Verlag, 1976), pp. 59-60.
30. Ladislaus Boros, *Aurelius Augustinus: Aufstieg zu Gott* (Freiburg: Walter-Verlag, 1982), p. 11.
31. D. T. Suzuki, *Essays in Zen Buddhism: First Series* (New York: Grove Press, 1961), p. 182.

32. Boros, *Aurelius Augustinus* p. 139.
33. *Walshe, *Meister Eckhart*, III, 67.
34. *Ibid., 55.
35. W. Y. Evans-Wentz, *The Tibetan Book of the Great Liberation* (London: Oxford University Press, 1954), p. 215, n. 4.
36. Torwesten, *Vedanta*, p. 27 (*Mundaka-Upanishad* II, 2, 10).
37. *Walshe, *Meister Eckhart*, III, 13-14.
38. Fritz Hungerleider, *Das Zen-Seminar* (Freiburg: Herder Verlag, 1976), p. 36.
39. Koun Yamada, *Die torlose Schranke: Mumonkan* (Munich: Kösel-Verlag, 1989), p. 289.

Chapter 4. FROM AN IMAGINED GOD
TO A NAMELESS DIVINITY

40. *Walshe, *Meister Eckhart*, III, p. 18.
41. Enomiya-Lassalle, *Zen und christliche Mystik*, p. 33.
42. *Walshe, *Meister Eckhart*, III, p. 128.
43. Willi Massa, ed., *Der Weg des Schweigens* (Kevelaer: Verlag Butzon & Bercker, 1984), p. 111.
44. Blofeld, *Huang Po*, pp. 62, 72.
45. *Walshe, *Meister Eckhart*, I, pp. 117-18.
46. Blofeld, *Huang Po*, p. 31.
47. Ibid., pp. 122-23.
48. Wolfgang Kopp, *Lao Tse: Tao-Te-King* (Interlaken: Ansata-Verlag, 1988), introduction.
49. Gerhard Wehr, *Esoterisches Christentum* (Stuttgart: Klett Verlag, 1975), p. 122.
50. K. O. Schmidt, *In Dir ist das Licht* (Munich: Drei-Eichen-Verlag, 1959), p. 108.
51. Govinda, *Creative Meditation*, p. 194.
52. D. T. Suzuki, *Essays in Zen Buddhism: Third Series* (London: Rider & Co./ Hutchinson Group, 1970), p. 67.
53. D. T. Suzuki, *An Introduction to Zen Buddhism* (New York: Grove Press, 1954), p. 46.
54. Ware, *Orthodox Way*, pp. 30-31.
55. Alan Watts, *Der Lauf des Wassers* (Munich: O. W. Barth Verlag, 1976), p. 131.
56. Anne Bancroft, *Zen* (Munich: Kösel-Verlag, 1985), pp. 15-16.

Chapter 5. THE WAY OF ACTIVE MEDITATION

57. Symeon der Theologe {Simeon the Theologian}, *Licht vom Licht* (Munich: Kösel-Verlag, 1951), p. 144.
58. Wehr, *Esoterisches Christentum*, p. 109.

59. Wehr, *Esoterisches Christentum*, p. 117.
60. Louise Gnädinger, ed., *Johannes Angelus Silesius: Cherubinischer Wandersmann* (Zurich: Manesse Verlag, 1986), p. 134.
61. Blofeld, *Huang Po*, p. 79.
62. *Walshe, I, 55, 59, and 61.
63. Garma C. C. Chang, *Die Praxis des Zen* (Freiburg: Aurum Verlag, 1982), p. 104.
64. Heinrich Zimmer, *Der Weg zum Selbst* (Düsseldorf: Diederichs Verlag, 1981), pp. 90-91.
65. Govinda, *Creative Meditation*, p. 65.
66. Ibid., p. 132.
67. Chang, *Zen*, p. 99.
68. Ibid., pp. 90-91.
69. *Walshe, *Meister Eckhart*, III, p. 17.
70. *Based upon the critical text of Phyllis Hodgson, ed., *The Cloud of Unknowing* and *The Book of Privy Counseling* (London: Oxford University Press, 1944), p. 126.
71. *F. C. Happold, *Mysticism: A Study and an Anthology* (Harmondsworth: Penguin Books, 1970), pp. 289-90.
72. Richard Garbe, ed., *Die Bhagavadgita* (Darmstadt: Wissenschaftliche Buchgesellschaft, 1978), pp. 125-26 (X 8, 10, 11).
73. Hugo M. Enomiya-Lassalle, *Zen-Unterweisung* (Munich: Kösel-Verlag, 1987), p. 13.
74. Karlfried Graf Dürckheim, *Mein Weg zur Mitte* (Freiburg: Herder Verlag, 1986), pp. 65-66.
75. Hans Joachim Stein, *Die Kunst des Bogenschießens-Kyudo* (Munich O. W. Barth Verlag, 1985), pp. 117-18.
76. Judith Blackstone, Zoran Josipovic, and Naomi Rosenblatt, *Zen für Anfänger* (Reinbek: Rowohlt Taschenbuch Verlag, 1987), p. 97.
77. Taisen Deshimaru, *Za-Zen* (Berlin: Kristkeitz Verlag, 1979), pp. 49-51.
78. Stein, *Kunst des Bogouschie Beus*, p. 118.
79. Detlef-I. Lauf, *Geheimlehren tibetischer Totenbücher* (Freiburg: Aurum Verlag, 1975), p. 226.
80. *Prabhavananda and Christopher Isherwood, trans., *The Song of God: Bhagavad-Gita* (New York: New American Library/Penguin USA, 1972), p. 75.
81. Garma C. C. Chang, *Mahamudra-Fibel* (Vienna: Octopus Verlag, 1979), p. 46.

Chapter 6. CRUCIFIXION AND TRANSFORMATION

82. K. O. Schmidt, *Meister Eckeharts Weg zum kosmischen Bewußtsein* (Munich: Drei-Eichen-Verlag, 1969), p. 127.

83. Boros, *Aurelius Augustinus*, p. 68.
84. Heinrich Dumoulin, *Östliche Meditation und christliche Mystik* (Freiburg: Verlag Karl Alber, 1966), p. 68.
85. Hugo M. Enomiya-Lassalle, *Zen-Meditation für Christen* (Munich: O. W. Barth Verlag, pp. 96-97.
86. Gnädinger, *Silesius*, p. 257.
87. Ibid., p. 46.
88. *Walshe, I, 118.
89. Gerhard Stenzel, ed., *Jakob Böhme: Leben und Werke* (n.p.: Mohn Verlag, n.d.), p. 184.
90. Gnädinger, *Silesius*, p. 85.
91. Gerhard Wehr, *Meister Eckhart* (Reinbek: Rowohlt Taschenbuch Verlag, 1989), pp.129-30.
92. Fritz Hungerleider, *Mein Weg zur Mystik* (Freiburg: Herder Verlag, 1988), p. 7.
93. Enomiya-Lassalle, *Zen-Meditation*, p. 96.
94. Schmidt, *Licht*, p. 148.
95. Ware, *Orthodox Way*, p. 29.
96. Heinrich Dumoulin, *Zen: Geschichte und Gestalt* (Bern: Francke Verlag, 1959), pp. 257-58.
97. Chang, *Zen*, p. 97.
98. Blofeld, *Huang Po*, pp. 32, 48.
99. Chang, *Zen*, pp. 98, 107.

Chapter 7. ASCENT TO LIGHT

100. *Happold, *Mysticism*, p. 291.
101. Schmidt, *Licht*, p. 7.
102. Le Saux, *Gegenwart*, p. 27 (Chandogya Upanishad 3, 13, 7).
103. Willi Massa, ed., *Die Höhle des Herzens* (Kevelaer: Verlag Butzon & Bercker, 1982), p. 17 (Mundaka Upanishad 3, 1, 7).
104. Schmidt, *Licht*, p. 10.
105. Ibid., p. 11.
106. Ibid., p. 12.
107. Dumoulin, *Zen*, p. 271.
108. *Walshe, *Meister Eckhart*, I, 154.
109. *Ibid., II, 87.
110. *Ibid., II, 276.
111. *Makoto Ueda, *Matsuo Basho* (Tokyo: Kodansha International, 1982), p. 53.
112. *Walshe, *Meister Eckhart*, III, 112.
113. *Based on Hodgson, *Cloud of Unknowing*, pp. 169-70.
114. *Walshe, *Meister Eckhart* II, 275.

Chapter 8. ENCOUNTER WITH THE MASTER

115. Glenn H. Mullin, *Death and Dying: The Tibetan Tradition* (London: Routledge & Kegan Paul, Arkana, 1986), p. 62.

116. D. T. Suzuki, *Erfülltes Leben aus Zen* (Munich: O. W. Barth Verlag, 1973), p. 223.

117. Ingrid Fischer-Schreiber et al., *The Encyclopedia of Eastern Philosophy and Religion* (Boston: Shambhala Publications, 1989), pp. 222-23.

118. Anne Bancroft, *Religionen des Ostens* (Zurich: Theseus Verlag, 1974), p. 145.

119. Namkhai Norbu, *The Crystal and the Way of Light* (New York: Routledge & Kegan Paul, 1987), p. 56.

120. Suzuki, *Essays: Third Series*, p. 47.

121. Prabhavananda and Manchester, *Upanishads*, p. 17.

122. Chang, *Zen*, pp. 34-36.

123. Jean Gebser, quoted in Lama Anagarika Govinda, *Buddhistische Reflexionen* (Munich: O. W. Barth Verlag, 1983), pp. 119-20.

124. Ibid., p. 120.

125. Blofeld, *Huang Po*, pp. 131-32.

126. Zenkei Shibayama, *A Flower Does Not Talk* (Rutland, Vt: Charles E. Tuttle, 1970), p. 171.

127. *Based on the following translations: Thomas à Kempis, *Of the Imitation of Christ* (London: Ward Lock, n. d.), pp. 56-59, and Thomas à Kempis, *The Imitation of Christ*, trans. William Benham, in *The Harvard Classics*, ed. Charles W. Elliot (New York: P. F. Collier, 1937), VII, 230-32.

128. Mullin, *Death and Dying*, p. 74.

129. Phillip Kapleau, *The Three Pillars of Zen* (New York: Anchor-Doubleday, 1989), p. 181.

130. Suzuki, *Introduction to Zen*, p. 47.

Chapter 9. THE ZEN WAY:
FREE YOURSELVES OF EVERYTHING

131. Shibayama, *A Flower Does Not Talk*, p. 76.

132. *D. T. Suzuki, *Living by Zen* (London: Rider-Random Century Group, 1991), p. 99.

133. Suzuki, *Essays: Third Series*, p. 54.

134. Ibid., pp. 55-56.

135. Ibid., p. 59.

136. Ibid., p. 59.

137. Ibid., p. 60.

138. Ibid., p. 60.

139. Ibid., p. 60.

140. Ibid., p. 61.
141. Ibid., p. 270.
142. Ibid., p. 270, n. 1.
143. Ibid., p. 271.
144. Ibid., p. 301.
145. Ibid., p. 301.
146. Blofeld, *Huang Po*, p. 61.
147. Chang, *Zen*, p. 88.
148. Chang, *Mahamudra*, pp. 53, 55.
149. Blofeld, *Huang Po*, pp. 36-37.
150. Zenkei Shibayama, *Zu den Quellen des Zen* (Munich: Heyne Verlag, 1986), p. 31.
151. W. Kopp, Mumonkan, *Koan* 1.
152. Shibayama, *Quellen des Zen*, p. 32.
153. Ibid., p. 21.
154. Fischer-Schreiber et al., *Encyclopedia*, p. 445.
155. Pierre Brun, trans., *Meister Linji—Begegnungen und Reden* (Zurich: Ammann Verlag, 1986), pp. 76, 65, 80.
156. Blackstone, Josipovic, and Rosenblatt, *Zen für Anfänger*, p. 158.